Paleo:

30 Day Paleo Challenge:

Discover the Secret to Health and Rapid Weight Loss with the Paleo 30 Day Challenge

Paleo Cookbook with Complete 30 Day Meal Plan

By: Brandon Solomon

30 Day Paleo Challenge

Legal notice

Table of Contents

Introduction

There are more miracle dieting programs available now than ever before. Despite that, obesity in the western world has never been worse. Our poor health and eating habits are becoming an existential threat. There are diets that have been around for decades that people still believe are the secret to slimming down. But in addition to those, we're seeing more and more fad diets appear every day. Most of these diets are aimed at helping people lose a lot of weight in a short span of time. There are many people that are trying to slim down and look 'perfect.' These people are sometimes even willing to take drugs or ingest pills that could harm the body to get that picture perfect body.

Is there any point in getting that skinny when you are sacrificing your health to do so? When it comes to dieting, you should really be looking for a diet that is healthy for you, not just one that will allow you to lose weight fast.

Before any of the current fad diets became popular, there was one diet that sustained the health and well-being of our ancestors for generations: Paleo. This diet offers not only a short timeline for losing weight but the diet will also help you stay fit while you're getting slimmer.

So why don't all diets give those results that they talk about? There are other factors to the success of a diet outside of what foods it requires you to cut out of your typical meals. You'll find that a diet is more successful if you're motivated, have discipline, and have attainable goals.

For this book, we'll be going through a 30-day Paleo meal plan that will help you to either start Paleo the right way, or reenergize your commitment to Paleo with an easy meal plan full of delicious, healthy recipes. If you're new to Paleo, this 30 day challenge might be all it takes to make you a convert for life. The meals included in this book won't require a ton of time to prepare and cook, but they will be simple and extremely delicious.

An Overview of Paleo

Paleo is all about going back to the diets of those in pre-historic times. Back then, people were more reliant on the environment for food. There wasn't a lot of cooking that happened at that point, so people were eating food without much if any processing.

These people, who had almost no cooking skills and limited knowledge about their health, survived in various environments. Even without the advanced medical knowledge that we have now, these people were able to thrive in that wild environment.

Things have changed since then, but Paleo has made a resurgence into the mainstream. This particular diet wants people to return to the ancient ways of eating. The point is to eat food with as little processing as possible. The diets from pre-historic times provided all the nutrients that we needed and lacked many of the extra sugars that have been added by modern processing of foods.

Paleo is specifically based on the idea of hunting and gathering. Foods like vegetables, fruits, nuts, seeds, meat, and fish are allowed in this diet. However, foods like dairy, grains, and most processed foods are entirely cut out of the diet because they are more modern inventions. Cutting out those foods should actually improve your body's ability to digest what you consume.

Paleo ensures that even when you're burning the fat in your body, you can still have enough energy to do everything that your day demands of you. Paleo takes into account everything that your body needs to thrive, such as having stable blood sugar and a good metabolism.

Reaching Your Ideal Body Weight and Improving Your Health

Slimming down some can improve your appearance and, in turn, improve your confidence. Because people want to feel good about themselves as soon as possible, many people choose to just cut down on how much they eat. However, simply cutting out as many calories as possible can create new problems for the body.

If you're eating less your body requires, you could potentially become nutrient deficient. When your body reaches this state, your metabolism doesn't work as well. While you may look the way you want for a little bit, your body will be inefficient about the food that you do consume. It can be extremely easy to pack back on those pounds that you spent so long shedding.

Paleo doesn't cut out everything. The diet focuses on getting your body nutrient rich foods. A meal made up of fruits and vegetables with a portion of meat or seafood with some oil can actually improve your health.

While this doesn't sound like it will work for weight loss, it really does. All the food you consume right now is either used for energy or turned into fat. In order to lose fat that is already on your body, you'll want to ensure that your body is not creating additional fat. You can do this by watching how many carbs you take in.

There's no way around eating carbs. The best that you can do for your diet is to watch how many carbs you are taking in and ensure the carbs you are consuming are high-quality, nutrient-dense, complex carbohydrates. When you've cut out as many bad carbs as possible, you'll find that your body will actually turn to the fat stores and chip away at those, turning them into extra energy. This is how you lose weight.

Weight loss with Paleo isn't about putting your body through hell. Your diet will work with your body and provide all the nutrients you need in a delicious meal. It may be the most enjoyable way that you have ever lost weight.

What You Can Eat on Paleo

This list covers most of the foods that you can eat during your Paleo challenge.

- Vegetables:
  Asparagus, artichoke, Brussels sprouts, broccoli, carrots, cabbages, cauliflower, chard, celery, collard green, cucumber, garlic, eggplant, green kale, ginger, lettuce, leek, onions, mushroom, pepper, parsnips, radishes, peas, spaghetti squash, spinach, yellow squash, sweet potato, tomato, and zucchini.

- Grass-Fed/Organic Meat and Fish:
  Turkey, chicken, duck, pork, grass-fed beef, lamb, goat, lobster, shrimps, tuna, clams, halibut, wild caught salmon, and scallops.

- Organic Eggs

- Nuts and Seeds:
  Pine Nuts, cashew, hazelnuts, walnuts, macadamia nuts, pumpkin seeds, sunflower seeds, pecans, and almonds.

- Fruits:
  Avocado, apple, peaches, papaya, pineapple, plums, blackberries, strawberries, raspberries, blueberries, grapes, mango, lemon, lime, lychee, watermelon, cantaloupe, figs, tangerines, banana, and oranges.

- Oils/Fats:
  Macadamia Oil, Olive Oil, Coconut Oil, Grass-fed Butter and Avocado Oil.

What You <u>Can't</u> Eat on Paleo

These are the foods that you should do your best to avoid while you are doing your Paleo challenge.

- Dairy:
  Non-fat dairy creamer, powdered milk, cheese, cream cheese, milk, yogurt, and powdered milk.

- Beverages:
  Soda, fruit juice with added sugar, coffee, and alcohol.

- Grains:
  Toast, wheat, pasta, crackers, breads, cereal, corn.

- Legumes:
  Broad beans, black beans, garbanzo beans, fava beans, horse beans, kidney beans, lima beans, navy beans, pinto beans, red beans, white beans, and string beans.

- Peas:
  Black-eyed peas, tofu, chickpeas, lentils, snow peas, soybeans, and peanuts.

- Artificial Sweeteners:
  Xylitol, Aspartame, and Saccharine.

- Snacks:
  Pretzels, chips, cookies, wheat thins, pastries, sun chips, and sweets.

Tips for a Paleo Beginner

Paleo is relatively simple, but nearly everyone finds that getting into a new diet is hard. In order to help you with your brand new diet, here are some tips that should help get you through your 30 day challenge.

Keep Your Food Simple
While it can be tempting to jump right into a diet, you'll want to avoid doing that. From the list of acceptable foods above, pick out the foods that you know you like and create meals with them. Branch out now and then to try new foods, but don't feel like you have to eat every single food on that list. Those are just suggestions for what you could be eating.

Drink Water
Whenever you feel thirsty, look for water. Water will benefit your body the most compared to other drinks out there. Don't drink calories.

Listen To Your Body
Your body will tell you what it wants and when. Often we eat out of boredom or compulsion. You need to learn to pay attention to hunger and ignore other reasons to eat. With practice, you will know when you are really hungry and when you just want to eat something for some other reason. You should respect your body and eat or drink until you feel satisfied. Just remember that the foods you reach for should be within the Paleo guidelines.

Be Patient
Paleo isn't just about the food that you're eating,
but about a lifestyle change. Your body will need
to take some time to adjust to all the changes
that you are making. If you are struggling with
the diet and cheat once or twice, then don't feel
bad about it. A little bit of a cheat day won't kill
you if it's only once in a while. The key is to get
back to the diet the next day and remember the
long term benefits that you want.

Find a Community
Trying a new diet can be hardest when you're
doing it alone. You can ask your partner, your
family, or your friends to try the diet with you.
When you have people in your life that are
involved in the same lifestyle, then it can be
easier to keep going. You'll be able to share
workout plans, recipes, and encourage anyone
that is struggling with the diet. In turn, someone
will be there to cheer you on when you feel like
you can't do it.

Day 1

Breakfast : Cinnamon Pumpkin Bread

Lunch : Sautéed Carrot Garlic

Dinner : Easy Baked Beef

Cinnamon Pumpkin Bread

Serving: 5

Nutrition Facts
Serving Size 5 (36g)
Per Serving

Calories 147
Total Fat 13.7g
Saturated Fat 10.8g
Trans Fat 0g
Cholesterol 65mg
Sodium 37mg
Potassium 24mg
Total Carb 3.8g
Dietary Fiber 2.4g
Sugars 0.5g
Protein 3.4g
Nutrition Facts
Serving Size 5 (36g)

Per Serving
Calories 147

Ingredients:

1 cup mashed pumpkin

2 organic eggs

18

¼ cup coconut oil

¼ cup coconut flour

1 teaspoon cinnamon powder

Directions:

- Preheat an oven to 350 °F then lines a small loaf with parchment paper. Set aside.
- Combine coconut flour with cinnamon powder then mix until combined. Set aside.
- Next, place mashed pumpkin in a mixing bowl and crack the organic eggs over the pumpkin.
- Pour coconut oil into the bowl then using a whisker, combine the three ingredients until incorporated.
- Add the dry mixture into the bowl then mix until completely combined.
- Pour the mixture into the prepared loaf then spread evenly.
- Bake for about 30 minutes until it sets and a stick inserted comes out clean.
- Remove the bread from the oven and let it cool for a few minutes.
- Take the bread out from the loaf pan then cut into slices.
- Arrange on a serving dish then serve.

Sautéed Carrot Garlic

Serving: 4

Nutrition Facts
Serving Size 4 (96g)
Per Serving
Calories 35
Total Fat 1.2g
Saturated Fat 1g
Trans Fat 0g
Cholesterol 0mg
Sodium 82mg
Potassium 188mg
Total Carb 5.9g
Dietary Fiber 2g
Sugars 3.2g
Protein 1g
Nutrition Facts
Serving Size 4 (96g)
Per Serving
Calories 35

Ingredients:

3 cups sliced carrots

¼ cup minced garlic

1 tablespoon chopped celery

¼ teaspoon pepper

1-teaspoon coconut oil

Directions:

- Preheat a skillet then pour coconut oil into it.

- Once it is hot, stir in minced garlic then sautés until wilted and aromatic.
- Next, add sliced carrots into the skillet then season with pepper. Keep stirring until the carrots are wilted and tender.
- After that, add celeries into the skillet then using a wooden spatula, mix all of them until combined and wilted.
- Transfer the carrots salads to a serving dish then enjoy warm.

Easy Baked Beef

Serving: 4

Nutrition Facts
Servings: 4
Per Serving
Calories 163
Total Fat 4.7g
Saturated Fat 2g
Trans Fat 0g
Cholesterol 80mg
Sodium 47mg
Potassium 13mg
Total Carb 0.7g
Dietary Fiber 0.2g
Sugars 0g
Protein 29.5g
Nutrition Facts
Servings: 4
Per Serving
Calories 163

Ingredients:

1 lb. grass-fed beef

¼ teaspoon cumin

¼ teaspoon oregano

1 teaspoon minced garlic

1-teaspoon black pepper

Directions:

- Combine cumin with oregano and minced garlic in a bowl.
- Rub the beef with the spice mixture then let it sit for about 10 minutes.

22

- Wrap the beef with aluminum foil then place in a baking sheet.
- Preheat an oven to 300 °F and once it is ready, place the baking sheet with wrapped beef in the oven. Bake for about an hour.
- When the process is done, remove the beef from the oven and carefully unwrap the beef.
- Place the baked beef on a serving dish then sprinkle black pepper on top.
- Serve and enjoy warm.

Day 2

Breakfast : Quick Almond Muffin

Lunch : Nutritious Cap Cay

Dinner : Warm Shrimp Curry

Quick Almond Muffin

Serving: 2

Nutrition Facts
Serving Size 2 (128g)
Per Serving

Calories 300
Total Fat 12.2g
Saturated Fat 8.2g
Trans Fat 0g
Cholesterol 164mg
Sodium 83mg
Potassium 59mg
Total Carb 37.7g
Dietary Fiber 2.9g
Sugars 0.8g
Protein 9.2g
Nutrition Facts
Serving Size 2 (128g)

Per Serving
Calories 300

Ingredients:

½ cup almond powder

2 tablespoons coconut flour

2 organic eggs

24

3 teaspoons coconut oil

¼ cup water

Directions:

- Prepare a microwave safe ramekin then greases with cooking spray. Set aside.
- Combine almond powder with coconut flour then stir until mixed.
- Crack the organic eggs then place in a mixing bowl.
- Add coconut oil into the bowl then pours water into it. Mix the liquid ingredients until incorporated.
- Next, add the dry mixture into the liquid mixture then mixes until combined.
- Pour the mixture into the greased ramekin then microwave on high for 2 minutes.
- Remove from the microwave then takes the muffins out from the ramekin.
- Serve and enjoy warm.

Nutritious Cap Cay

Serving: 2

Nutrition Facts
Serving Size 4 (175g)
Per Serving
Calories 104
Total Fat 4.1g
Saturated Fat 2.5g
Trans Fat 0g
Cholesterol 19mg
Sodium 46mg
Potassium 405mg
Total Carb 9.6g
Dietary Fiber 2.2g
Sugars 3.2g
Protein 8.4g
Nutrition Facts
Serving Size 4 (175g)
Per Serving
Calories 104

Ingredients:

2 cups cauliflower florets

½ cup sliced carrots

1 cup chopped organic chicken breast

¼ cup minced garlic

¼ teaspoon pepper

2 teaspoons coconut oil

1 medium cucumber, for garnish

Directions:

- Preheat a skillet then pour coconut oil into it.
- Once it is hot, stir in minced garlic then sautés until aromatic and lightly golden brown.
- Next, add chopped chicken breast into the skillet then sautés until the chicken is no longer pink.
- Add carrots and cauliflower florets then season with pepper. Stir for a few minutes until the vegetables are wilted and the chicken is completely cooked.
- Transfer the cooked cap cay to a serving dish then garnishes with sliced cucumber around the dish.
- Serve and enjoy warm.

Warm Shrimps Curry

Serving: 6

Nutrition Facts
Servings: 6
Per Serving
Calories 228
Total Fat 20.4g
Saturated Fat 17.7g
Trans Fat 0g
Cholesterol 60mg
Sodium 83mg
Potassium 280mg
Total Carb 5.7g
Dietary Fiber 2g
Sugars 2.7g
Protein 8.4g
Nutrition Facts
Servings: 6
Per Serving
Calories 228

Ingredients:

2 cups fresh shrimps

1 tablespoon sliced shallot

1 teaspoon minced garlic

½ teaspoon curry

½ teaspoon turmeric

1 teaspoon red chili flakes

½ teaspoon pepper

2 cups coconut milk

1-teaspoon coconut oil

1 tablespoon chopped celery

Directions:

- Peel the fresh shrimps then place in a bowl.
- Preheat a wok over medium heat then pour coconut oil into it.
- Once it is hot, stir in sliced shallot and minced garlic then sautés until aromatic.
- Add curry and turmeric into the wok then toss in peeled shrimps then stir vigorously.
- Pour coconut milk into the wok then sprinkle pepper and red chili flakes on top. Bring to boil then cook the shrimps for a few minutes.
- Transfer to a serving bowl then enjoy hot.

Day 3

Breakfast : Banana Muffins with Ginger

Lunch   : Zucchini Tuna Salads

Dinner   : Chicken Balls with Thick Gravy

Banana Muffins with Ginger

Serving: 6

Nutrition Facts
Serving Size 6 (129g)
Per Serving
Calories 98
Total Fat 4.2g
Saturated Fat 2.7g
Trans Fat 0g
Cholesterol 82mg
Sodium 61mg
Potassium 54mg
Total Carb 9.7g
Dietary Fiber 5.2g
Sugars 2g
Protein 4.9g
Nutrition Facts
Serving Size 6 (129g)
Per Serving
Calories 98

Ingredients:

6 tablespoons coconut flour

4 tablespoons mashed banana

3 organic eggs

½ teaspoon cinnamon powder

½ teaspoon ginger powder

½ teaspoon lemon juice

Directions:

- Preheat an oven to 350 °F then greases 6 muffin cups. Set aside.
- Place all ingredients in a bowl then using a whisker, combine until incorporated.
- Divide the mixture into 6 prepared muffin cups then bake for about 25 minutes until the muffins are set and completely cooked.
- Once it is done, remove from the oven then let them cool.
- Serve and enjoy.

Zucchini Tuna Salads

Serving: 4

Nutrition Facts
Serving Size 4 (149g)
Per Serving
Calories 97
Total Fat 2.9g
Saturated Fat 0.8g
Trans Fat 0g
Cholesterol 21mg
Sodium 32mg
Potassium 406mg
Total Carb 3.8g
Dietary Fiber 1.2g
Sugars 2g
Protein 14g
Nutrition Facts
Serving Size 4 (149g)
Per Serving
Calories 97

Ingredients:

1 cup cooked tuna

2 medium zucchini

1-tablespoon lemon juice

2 tablespoons chopped onion

Directions:

- Peel and shred the zucchini then place in a salad bowl.
- Add cooked tuna into the bowl then sprinkle chopped onion over the tuna.

- Drizzle lemon juice then using two forks mix the salads until well combined.
- Transfer the salads to a container with a lid then chills in the refrigerator for at least an hour.
- Once you want to consume it, remove from the refrigerator and enjoy right away.

Chicken Balls with Thick Gravy

Serving: 6

Nutrition Facts
Serving Size 6 (222g)
Per Serving

Calories 200
Total Fat 16.4g
Saturated Fat 13.5g
Trans Fat 0g
Cholesterol 13mg
Sodium 414mg
Potassium 321mg
Total Carb 5.7g
Dietary Fiber 2.3g
Sugars 2.7g
Protein 9g
Nutrition Facts
Serving Size 6 (222g)
Per Serving
Calories 200

Ingredients:

1 lb. organic chicken breast

1-tablespoon coconut flour

1 organic egg white

2 teaspoons minced garlic

3 cups water

1-teaspoon coconut oil

1 tablespoon chopped onion

1 teaspoon red chili

1 ½ cup coconut milk

Directions:

- Place the chicken breast in a food processor together with coconut flour and a teaspoon of minced garlic. Pulse the processor until smooth.
- Transfer the mixture to a bowl then add egg white into it. Using your hand, mix until combined.
- Shape the mixture into medium balls form.
- Meanwhile, pour water into a pot then brings to boil.
- Once it is boiled, add the meatballs into the pot then cook until the balls floating.
- Strain the cooked chicken balls then set aside.
- Preheat a saucepan over medium heat then pour coconut oil into it.
- Stir in chopped onion and red chili into the saucepan then sautés until wilted.
- Pour coconut milk into the saucepan and add the chicken balls into it.
- Bring to a simmer for about 5 minutes then transfer the cook chicken balls together with the gravy to the bowl.
- Serve and enjoy hot.

Day 4

Breakfast : Spicy Frittata Muffins

Lunch : Avocado Veggie Salads

Dinner : Red Hot Chicken

Spicy Frittata Muffins

Serving: 6

Nutrition Facts
Serving Size 2 (64g)
Per Serving
Calories 72
Total Fat 5g
Saturated Fat 1.9g
Trans Fat 0g
Cholesterol 164mg
Sodium 68mg
Potassium 131mg
Total Carb 1.2g
Dietary Fiber 0.4g
Sugars 0.7g
Protein 5.9g
Nutrition Facts
Serving Size 2 (64g)
Per Serving
Calories 72

Ingredients:

6 organic eggs

1 cup chopped broccoli

½ cup sliced red chili

¾ teaspoon pepper

¼ teaspoon coconut oil

Directions:

- Preheat an oven to 400 °F then brushes six muffin cups with coconut oil. Set aside.
- Crack the eggs then place in a bowl.
- Season with pepper then add chopped broccoli and red chili. Stir well.
- Pour the egg mix into the prepared muffin cups then bake for 15 minutes.
- Once it is done, remove the baked egg from the oven then let them warm for a few minutes.
- Serve and enjoy warm.

Avocado Veggie Salads

Serving: 4

Nutrition Facts
Servings: 4
Per Serving
Calories 128
Total Fat 10.1g
Saturated Fat 2.2g
Trans Fat 0g
Cholesterol 0mg
Sodium 10mg
Potassium 513mg
Total Carb 9.9g
Dietary Fiber 4.5g
Sugars 3.2g
Protein 2g
Nutrition Facts
Servings: 4
Per Serving
Calories 128

Ingredients:

1 ripe avocado

1 medium cucumber

3 red tomatoes

2 cups chopped lettuce

2 tablespoons lemon juice

Directions:

- Peel the avocado then discard the seed. Cut the avocado into cubes then place in a salad bowl.

- Discard the cucumber seeds then cut into thick slices. Toss in the cucumber into the salad bowl then move to other vegetable.
- Chop the red tomatoes into the salad bowl as well then add lettuce into it.
- Drizzle lemon juice over the salad then using two forks mix all of the ingredients until well combined.
- Chill in the refrigerator for at least an hour then enjoy whenever you want.

Red Hot Chicken

Serving: 5

Nutrition Facts
Servings: 4
Per Serving
Calories 212
Total Fat 5.9g
Saturated Fat 3g
Trans Fat 0g
Cholesterol 87mg
Sodium 79mg
Potassium 336mg
Total Carb 4.9g
Dietary Fiber 0.5g
Sugars 1g
Protein 33.7g
Nutrition Facts
Servings: 4
Per Serving
Calories 212

Ingredients:

1 lb. organic chicken

2 cloves garlic

3 tablespoons chopped shallot

½ cup red chilies

½ teaspoon turmeric

2 teaspoons lemon grass

2 teaspoons crumbled bay leaves

2 teaspoons coconut oil

2 cups water

Directions:

- Place garlic, shallot, and red chilies in a food processor then pulse until smooth.
- Preheat a wok over medium heat then pour coconut oil into it.
- Once it is hot, stir in the garlic, shallot, and chilies mixture into the wok together with turmeric, lemon grass, and bay leaves. Sauté until aromatic.
- Pour water into the wok then add chicken into it.
- Stir occasionally then brings to boil until the water is completely absorbed into the chicken.
- When the chicken is completely cooked, transfer to a serving dish then enjoys.

Day 5

Breakfast : Coconut Zucchini Bread

Lunch : Beef Coconut Burritos

Dinner : Cabbage Soup

Coconut Zucchini Bread

Serving: 16

Nutrition Facts
Serving Size 16 (87g)
Per Serving
Calories 57
Total Fat 3.8g
Saturated Fat 2.4g
Trans Fat 0g
Cholesterol 61mg
Sodium 34mg
Potassium 150mg
Total Carb 3.3g
Dietary Fiber 1.5g
Sugars 1.2g
Protein 3.1g
Nutrition Facts
Serving Size 16 (87g)
Per Serving
Calories 57

Ingredients:

4 medium zucchini

3 cups coconut flour

42

6 organic eggs

2 tablespoons coconut oil

1 tablespoon cinnamon powder

Directions:

- Preheat an oven to 350 °F then lines two medium loaf pans with parchment paper. Set aside.
- Peel the zucchinis then shred them and place in a bowl.
- Add the eggs into the bowl together with coconut oil then season with cinnamon.
- After that, stir in coconut flour into the mixture then mix until completely combined.
- Pour the mixture into two prepared loaf pans then spread evenly.
- Bake the bread for about 50 minutes until set and lightly brown on top.
- Remove from the oven and let them cool for a few minutes.
- Cut the bread into slices and serve warm.

Beef Coconut Burritos

Serving: 4

Nutrition Facts
Serving Size 4 (191g)
Per Serving
Calories 206
Total Fat 10.2g
Saturated Fat 5.6g
Trans Fat 0g
Cholesterol 250mg
Sodium 81mg
Potassium 101mg
Total Carb 6.1g
Dietary Fiber 2.8g
Sugars 1.3g
Protein 22.2g
Nutrition Facts
Serving Size 4 (191g)
Per Serving
Calories 206

Ingredients:

TORTILLAS:

2 tablespoons coconut flour

4 organic egg whites

4 tablespoons water

1-teaspoon coconut oil

STUFFING:

1-teaspoon coconut oil

½ lb. grass-fed beef

¼ cup chopped onion

2 tablespoons diced tomato

1 teaspoon minced garlic

4 organic egg yolks

2 tablespoons water

¼ teaspoon pepper

Directions:

- Combine all of the tortillas ingredients except coconut oil in bowl then mix until completely incorporated.
- Preheat a skillet over medium heat then once it is hot, brush the skillet with coconut oil then pour half of the mixture into the pan.
- Swirl the pan to make the mixture spread evenly then cook it for about 2 minutes.
- Flip the tortilla then cooks for another 2 minutes until both sides are well cooked.
- Repeat with the remaining ingredients then set aside.
- Mince the grass-fed beef then set aside.
- Preheat a saucepan then pour coconut oil into it.
- Stir in chopped onion and minced garlic into the pan the sautés until wilted and aromatic.
- Add the minced beef then stirs until the beef is completely seasoned.
- Pour the egg yolks over the beef then scrambles until the egg sets.
- Add water into the pan then cooks for about three minutes until the water is completely absorbed into the beef.
- Add diced tomatoes into the pan then season with pepper. Stir well.

- Place the tortillas on a flat surface then drop the stuffing on them.
- Roll each tortilla tightly then serve on a serving dish.
- Enjoy!

Cabbage Light Soup

Serving: 4

Nutrition Facts
Servings: 4

Per Serving

Calories 66
Total Fat 1.8g
Saturated Fat 0.5g
Trans Fat 0g
Cholesterol 0mg
Sodium 973mg
Potassium 382mg
Total Carb 5.3g
Dietary Fiber 1.4g
Sugars 3g
Protein 6.7g
Nutrition Facts

Servings: 4

Per Serving
Calories 66

Ingredients:

2 cups chopped cabbage

1 cup cubed carrot

1 teaspoon chopped celery

5 cups vegetable broth

¼ teaspoon pepper

¼ teaspoon nutmeg

1 tablespoon chopped onion

Directions:

- Pour vegetable broth in a pot.

- Add chopped onion into the pot then bring to boil.
- Once it is boiled, stir in chopped cabbage and carrot into the pot then season with pepper and nutmeg.
- Stir the soup occasionally and bring to a simmer for about 3 minutes.
- When the vegetables are wilted and cooked, remove from heat then transfer the soup to serving bowl.
- Sprinkle chopped celery over the soup then enjoy hot.

Day 6

Breakfast : Original Almond Pancakes

Lunch : Beef Meatball Tomato

Dinner : Tuna in Tomato Bowl

Original Almond Pancakes

Serving: 2

Nutrition Facts
Serving Size 2 (125g)
Per Serving

Calories 374
Total Fat 34.8g
Saturated Fat 10g
Trans Fat 0g
Cholesterol 246mg
Sodium 97mg
Potassium 167mg
Total Carb 4.7g
Dietary Fiber 2.2g
Sugars 2g
Protein 9g
Nutrition Facts
Serving Size 2 (125g)

Per Serving
Calories 374

Ingredients:

2 tablespoons almond oil

3 organic eggs

49

4 tablespoons almond milk

4 tablespoons almond flour

Directions:

- Combine almond oil with almond milk then stir well.
- Crack the eggs then place in another bowl.
- Lightly beat the eggs then pour the beaten eggs into the liquid mixture.
- After that, add almond flour into the liquid mixture and mix until incorporated.
- Preheat a pan then coat with cooking oil.
- Once it is hot, pour about two tablespoons of the mixture into the pan and spread evenly.
- Cook for about 2 minutes until bubbles then flip the pancake and cook for another 2 minutes until both sides are brown.
- Transfer the cooked pancake to a serving platter then repeat with the remaining mixture.
- Serve and enjoy warm.

Beef Meatballs in Tomato Sauce

Serving: 3

Nutrition Facts
Serving Size 3 (220g)
Per Serving
Calories 347
Total Fat 23.8g
Saturated Fat 9.4g
Trans Fat 0g
Cholesterol 235mg
Sodium 140mg
Potassium 268mg
Total Carb 5.5g
Dietary Fiber 1.2g
Sugars 2.7g
Protein 27.9g
Nutrition Facts
Serving Size 3 (220g)
Per Serving
Calories 347

Ingredients:

¾ lb. grass-fed ground beef

3 organic eggs

1 teaspoon minced garlic

¼ teaspoon nutmeg

¼ teaspoon ginger

1 ½ teaspoons almond meal

½ teaspoon coconut oil

SAUCE:

½ teaspoon vegetable oil

2 tablespoons chopped onion

½ cup tomato puree

¼ teaspoon pepper

2 tablespoons watei

Directions:

- Place ground beef in a bowl then season with minced garlic and pepper. Stir well.
- Add almond meal into the mixture then using your hand, combine the mixture.
- Next, crack the egg and drop it over the turkey then mix until completely combined.
- After that, shape the mixture into small balls form then let them sit in the refrigerator for about 5 minutes.
- Meanwhile, preheat a pan over low heat then pour coconut oil into it.
- Place the meatballs on the pan then cooks for about 4 minutes then flip it.
- Cook the meatballs for another 4 minutes until both sides are brown and completely cooked.
- Transfer the cooked meatballs on a serving dish. Set aside.
- Next, preheat a saucepan over medium heat then pour vegetable oil into it.
- Stir in chopped onion then sautés until translucent and aromatic.
- Add tomato puree and water into the saucepan then season with pepper. Stir until completely mixed.
- Bring to a simmer until the sauce is completely cooked and thickened.

- Pour the sauce over the meatballs then serve warm.

Tuna in Tomato Bowl

Serving. 4

Nutrition Facts
Serving Size 3 (220g)
Per Serving
Calories 347
Total Fat 23.8g
Saturated Fat 9.4g
Trans Fat 0g
Cholesterol 235mg
Sodium 140mg
Potassium 268mg
Total Carb 5.5g
Dietary Fiber 1.2g
Sugars 2.7g
Protein 27.9g
Nutrition Facts
Serving Size 3 (220g)
Per Serving
Calories 347

Ingredients:

4 large red tomatoes

3 cups cooked tuna

1-teaspoon coconut oil

¾ cup coconut milk

¼ cup chopped onion

½ teaspoon pepper

Celeries, for garnish

Directions:

- Preheat a skillet over medium heat then pour coconut oil into it.
- Once it is hot, stir in chopped onion then sautés until wilted and aromatic.
- Add tuna into the skillet then pour coconut milk over the skillet. Stir until the coconut milk is completely absorbed into the tuna.
- Season with pepper then keeps stirring until the tuna is completely seasoned.
- Preheat an oven to 400 °F then lines a baking sheet with parchment paper. Set aside.
- Cut the top of the tomatoes then discard the pulp until the tomatoes becoming small bowls.
- Fill each tomato with cooked tuna then arranges on the prepared baking sheet.
- Bake the filled tomatoes for about 15 minutes and once it is done, take them out from the oven.
- Transfer the stuffed tomatoes on a serving dish then garnish with celery.
- Serve and enjoy warm.

Day 7

Breakfast : Savory Coconut Waffles

Lunch : Green Almond Salads

Dinner : Baked Salmon with Mushroom and Broccoli

Savory Coconut Waffles

Serving: 2

Nutrition Facts
Serving Size 2 (203g)
Per Serving
Calories 203
Total Fat 9.1g
Saturated Fat 3g
Trans Fat 0g
Cholesterol 327mg
Sodium 166mg
Potassium 405mg
Total Carb 17.7g
Dietary Fiber 3.3g
Sugars 4.8g
Protein 13.1g
Nutrition Facts
Serving Size 2 (203g)
Per Serving
Calories 203

Ingredients:

2 medium sweet potatoes

4 organic eggs

¼ cup coconut flour

½ cup chopped onion

1 tablespoon lemon juice

2 tablespoons chopped cilantro

¼ teaspoon pepper

Directions:

- Peel and shred the sweet potatoes then place in a bowl.
- Next, crack the eggs then add them into the same bowl with the shredded sweet potatoes.
- Add coconut flour into the bowl together with chopped onion, lemon juice, cilantro, and pepper then mix until combined.
- Preheat a waffle iron and once it is hot, pour the mixture into the iron and cook according to the waffle iron's instructions.
- Repeat with the remaining ingredients then arrange the waffles on a serving dish.
- Enjoy warm!

Green Almond Salads

Serving: 2

Nutrition Facts
Serving Size 2 (173g)
Per Serving
Calories 251
Total Fat 14.1g
Saturated Fat 3.8g
Trans Fat 0g
Cholesterol 28mg
Sodium 50mg
Potassium 467mg
Total Carb 4.8g
Dietary Fiber 1.8g
Sugars 1.5g
Protein 25.9g
Nutrition Facts
Serving Size 2 (173g)
Per Serving
Calories 251

Ingredients:

1 cup minced tuna

2 cups chopped lettuce

3 tablespoons chopped almond

1-tablespoon lemon juice

2 tablespoons chopped onion

¼ teaspoon pepper

1-teaspoon coconut oil

Directions:

- Preheat a saucepan over medium heat then pour coconut oil into it.
- Once it is hot, stir in minced tuna into the saucepan then season with pepper.
- Sauté the tuna until it completely seasoned and cooked.
- Transfer the cooked tuna into the bowl then sprinkle chopped onion over the tuna.
- Add chopped lettuce and almonds into the bowl then drizzles lemon juice over the ingredients.
- Using two forks mix the salads until well combined.
- Transfer the salads to a container with a lid then chills in the refrigerator for at least an hour.
- Once you want to consume it, remove from the refrigerator and enjoy right away.

Baked Salmon with Mushroom and Broccoli

Serving: 2

Nutrition Facts
Servings: 4

Per Serving

Calories 196
Total Fat 9.5g
Saturated Fat 3g
Trans Fat 0g
Cholesterol 50mg
Sodium 62mg
Potassium 613mg
Total Carb 5.4g
Dietary Fiber 1.1g
Sugars 0.9g
Protein 23.8g
Nutrition Facts

Servings: 4

Per Serving
Calories 196

Ingredients:

1 lb. Salmon fillet

1-teaspoon black pepper

1 tablespoon lemon juice

1-cup broccoli florets

1 cup chopped mushroom

1 tablespoon chopped celery

¼ cup minced garlic

2 teaspoons coconut oil

Directions:

- Preheat an oven to 350 °F then prepares a baking sheet.
- Place the salmon fillet in a bowl then sprinkle pepper over the salmon.
- Drizzle a teaspoon of coconut oil then splashes lemon juice over the salmon. Rub until the salmon is completely seasoned.
- Wrap the seasoned salmon with aluminum foil then place on the prepared baking sheet.
- Bake the salmon for about 40 minutes until completely cooked.
- Meanwhile, preheat a skillet then pour coconut oil into it.
- Once it is hot, stir in minced garlic then sautés until wilted and aromatic.
- Next, add broccoli florets and chopped mushroom into the skillet. Stir until the broccoli and mushroom are wilted and tender. Remove from heat and set aside.
- When the salmon is completely cooked, take it out from the oven then carefully unwrap it.
- Transfer the baked salmon to a serving dish then pour sautéed broccoli and mushroom over the salmon.
- Sprinkle celeries on top then serves warm.

Day 8

Breakfast : Healthy Granola Mix

Lunch : Nutritious Cauliflower Bites

Dinner : Fresh Savory Shrimps

Healthy Granola Mix

Serving: 2

Nutrition Facts
Serving Size 2 (103g)
Per Serving
Calories 575
Total Fat 52.7g
Saturated Fat 20g
Trans Fat 0g
Cholesterol 0mg
Sodium 27mg
Potassium 157mg
Total Carb 14.6g
Dietary Fiber 8.2g
Sugars 3.5g
Protein 5.5g
Nutrition Facts
Serving Size 2 (103g)
Per Serving
Calories 575

Ingredients:

¾ cup almond flour

2-½ tablespoons coconut oil

62

1 teaspoon cinnamon powder

1-teaspoon nutmeg

¼ cup chopped walnuts

½ cup grated coconut

¼ cup hemp seeds

Directions:

- Preheat an oven to 275 °F then lines a baking sheet with parchment paper. Set aside.
- Place all ingredients in a bowl then stir until well mixed.
- Spread the mixture on the prepared baking sheet then bakes for 40 minutes until the mixture is completely toasted.
- Once it is done, remove from the oven and let them cool.
- Save the toasted granola in a container with a lid and enjoy anytime you want.

Nutritious Cauliflower Bites

Serving: 2

Nutrition Facts
Serving Size 2 (103g)
Per Serving
Calories 101
Total Fat 6.3g
Saturated Fat 2.4g
Trans Fat 0g
Cholesterol 164mg
Sodium 78mg
Potassium 244mg
Total Carb 5g
Dietary Fiber 1.7g
Sugars 1.7g
Protein 7.1g
Nutrition Facts
Serving Size 2 (103g)
Per Serving
Calories 101

Ingredients:

1-½ cup cauliflower florets

1 tablespoon chopped leek

2 organic eggs

2 teaspoons minced garlic

½ teaspoon pepper

1 ½ teaspoons almond meal

½ teaspoon coconut oil

Directions:

- Place cauliflower florets in a food processor together minced garlic and pepper. Stir well.
- Add almond meal and chopped leek into the mixture then using your hand, combine the mixture.
- Next, crack the egg and drop it over the cauliflower mixture then mix until completely combined.
- Preheat a pan over low heat then pour coconut oil into it.
- Drop a scoop of the mixture on the preheated saucepan then cook for another 4 minutes until both sides are brown and completely cooked.
- Transfer the cooked cauliflower bites on a serving dish then serves.
- Enjoy warm.

Savory Fresh Shrimps

Serving: 4

Nutrition Facts
Serving Size 4 (96g)
Per Serving
Calories 35
Total Fat 1.2g
Saturated Fat 1g
Trans Fat 0g
Cholesterol 0mg
Sodium 82mg
Potassium 188mg
Total Carb 5.9g
Dietary Fiber 2g
Sugars 3.2g
Protein 1g
Nutrition Facts
Serving Size 4 (96g)
Per Serving
Calories 35

Ingredients:

2 cups medium fresh shrimps

¼ cup minced garlic

¼ teaspoon pepper

2 teaspoons coconut oil

1 tablespoon lemon juice

Directions:

- Splash lemon juice over the shrimps then rub for a few minutes. Set aside.

- Preheat a skillet then pour coconut oil into it.
- Once it is hot, stir in minced garlic then sautés until wilted and aromatic.
- Next, toss in the fresh shrimps into the skillet then season with pepper. Keep stirring until the shrimps are pink.
- Transfer the sautéed shrimps to a serving dish then enjoy warm.

Day 9

Breakfast : Mixed Cereal with Sliced Banana

Lunch : Energizing Salads

Dinner : Spicy Beef in Coconut Gravy

Mixed Cereal with Sliced Banana

Serving: 4

Nutrition Facts
Serving Size 3 (147g)
Per Serving
Calories 306
Total Fat 21.7g
Saturated Fat 10g
Trans Fat 0g
Cholesterol 0mg
Sodium 109mg
Potassium 420mg
Total Carb 28g
Dietary Fiber 6.4g
Sugars 13.6g
Protein 8.6g
Nutrition Facts
Serving Size 3 (147g)
Per Serving
Calories 306

Ingredients:

¼ cup roasted sliced almonds

¼ cup roasted pumpkin seeds

2 tablespoons chia seeds

½ cup coconut milk

½ cup water

2 ripe bananas

Directions:

- Place chia seeds in a bowl then pour coconut oil and water into it. Let it sit for about 5 minutes until the chia seeds are thicken.
- Meanwhile, place the almonds and pumpkin seeds in a food processor then pulse for several times until the almond and pumpkin seeds are crumbled.
- Next, transfer the almonds and pumpkin seeds to the thickened chia seeds then mix well.
- Cut the bananas into slices then arranges them over the cereal.
- Serve and enjoy immediately.

Energizing Salads

Serving: 6

Nutrition Facts
Serving Size 6 (160g)
Per Serving
Calories 125
Total Fat 5.2g
Saturated Fat 2g
Trans Fat 0g
Cholesterol 107mg
Sodium 120mg
Potassium 254mg
Total Carb 5.3g
Dietary Fiber 2g
Sugars 2.5g
Protein 12.5g
Nutrition Facts
Serving Size 6 (160g)
Per Serving
Calories 125

Ingredients:

3 medium carrots

2 cups chopped organic chicken breast

2 cups chopped spinach, or any green you like

2 cups chopped lettuce, or any green you like

½ cup cherry tomatoes

3 organic eggs

2 tablespoons lemon juice

1-teaspoon coconut oil

¼ teaspoon pepper

Directions:

- Pour water in a pot then boil the organic eggs. Once it is boiled, discard the hot water then soak the boiled eggs in cold water.
- When the boiled eggs are cold, peel the eggs then set aside.
- Peel carrots then shred them.
- Place the shredded carrots in a steamer then steam until tender. Set aside.
- After that, preheat a skillet then pour coconut oil into it.
- Once the oil is hot, stir in chopped organic chicken breast then sauté until wilted.
- Season with pepper and cook the chicken well.
- Arrange cooked chicken, steamed carrots, chopped spinach, chopped lettuce, boiled eggs, and cherry tomatoes on a serving dish.
- Drizzle lemon juice over the salads then enjoy right away.

Spicy Beef in Coconut Gravy

Serving: 10

Nutrition Facts
Servings: 10
Per Serving
Calories 217
Total Fat 16.1g
Saturated Fat 12.3g
Trans Fat 0g
Cholesterol 36mg
Sodium 41mg
Potassium 354mg
Total Carb 5g
Dietary Fiber 1.7g
Sugars 2.4g
Protein 14.4g
Nutrition Facts
Servings: 10
Per Serving
Calories 217

Ingredients:

1 lb. grass-fed beef

Papaya leaves, for wrapping

2 cloves garlic

3 tablespoons chopped shallot

½ cup red chilies

½ teaspoon turmeric

2 teaspoons lemon grass

2 teaspoons crumbled bay leaves

2 teaspoons coconut oil

2 cups water

2 cups coconut milk

Celeries, for garnish

Directions:

- Cut the grass-fed beef into medium cubes then wrap using papaya leaves. Let it sit for about 20 minutes—this will help the beef to be soft easier in a short period of cooking.
- Unwrap the papaya leaves then wash and rinse the beef.
- Place garlic, shallot, and red chilies in a food processor then pulse until smooth.
- Preheat a wok over medium heat then pour coconut oil into it.
- Once it is hot, stir in the garlic, shallot, and chilies mixture into the wok together with turmeric, lemon grass, and bay leaves. Sauté until aromatic.
- Pour water into the wok then add the beef into it.
- Stir occasionally then brings to boil until the water is reduced into half and the beef is completely seasoned.
- Pour coconut milk into the skillet then bring to boil while stirring occasionally.
- When the beef is completely cooked, transfer to a serving dish together with the coconut gravy.
- Garnish with celeries then serve warm.

Day 10

Breakfast : Refreshing Scrambled Egg

Lunch : Chicken in Egg Burritos

Dinner : Green Kale Garlic

Refreshing Scrambled Egg

Serving: 1

Nutrition Facts
Serving Size 1 (186g)
Per Serving
Calories 194
Total Fat 11.4g
Saturated Fat 4.7g
Trans Fat 0g
Cholesterol 327mg
Sodium 127mg
Potassium 381mg
Total Carb 12.4g
Dietary Fiber 2.4g
Sugars 7.7g
Protein 12.3g
Nutrition Facts
Serving Size 1 (186g)
Per Serving
Calories 194

Ingredients:

½ teaspoon coconut oil

¼ cup chopped kiwi

½ cup chopped bell pepper

74

2 organic eggs

½ teaspoon black pepper

Directions:

- Crack the organic eggs then place on a bowl.
- Season with pepper then stir well.
- Preheat a saucepan over medium heat then pour coconut oil into it.
- Add chopped bell pepper into the saucepan then stir until wilted.
- Pour the beaten egg into the saucepan then quickly scramble the egg.
- After that, add chopped kiwi into the saucepan then stir until just combined.
- Transfer the scrambled egg to a serving dish then enjoy warm.

Chicken in Egg Burritos

Serving: 2

Nutrition Facts
Serving Size 2 (206g)
Per Serving
Calories 249
Total Fat 13.5g
Saturated Fat 4.3g
Trans Fat 0g
Cholesterol 449mg
Sodium 191mg
Potassium 366mg
Total Carb 7.2g
Dietary Fiber 1.6g
Sugars 2.7g
Protein 24.2g
Nutrition Facts
Serving Size 2 (206g)
Per Serving
Calories 249

Ingredients:

4 organic egg whites

4 organic egg yolks

½ cup chopped onion

1-teaspoon olive oil

¼ cup diced tomato

2 tablespoons diced chili

1-tablespoon cilantro

½ cup cooked shredded chicken

Directions:

- Place the egg whites in a bowl then whisk until beaten.
- Preheat a medium skillet then coat with cooking oil.
- Pour about half of the egg whites into the pan swirl around so the egg whites will spread evenly.
- Cook for about 2 minutes then flip it until both sides are lightly golden brown.
- Repeat with the remaining egg whites then set aside.
- Next, preheat a skillet then pour olive oil in it.
- Stir in onion then sautés until wilted and aromatic.
- Add diced tomato and chili then after that stir in cilantro and shredded chicken.
- Sauté until all of them are wilted then pour beaten egg yolks into the skillet.
- Scramble the egg and mix with the chicken and vegetables.
- Place the egg whites tortillas on a flat surface then drop the chicken mixture on them.
- Roll each tortilla tightly then place on a serving dish.
- Serve and enjoy!

Green Kale Garlic

Serving: 4

Nutrition Facts
Serving Size 4 (96g)
Per Serving
Calories 35
Total Fat 1.2g
Saturated Fat 1g
Trans Fat 0g
Cholesterol 0mg
Sodium 82mg
Potassium 188mg
Total Carb 5.9g
Dietary Fiber 2g
Sugars 3.2g
Protein 1g
Nutrition Facts
Serving Size 4 (96g)
Per Serving
Calories 35

Ingredients:

4 cups chopped kale

¼ cup minced garlic

¼ teaspoon pepper

1-teaspoon coconut oil

Directions:

- Preheat a skillet then pour coconut oil into it.
- Once it is hot, stir in minced garlic then sautés until aromatic and lightly golden brown.

78

- Next, add chopped kale into the skillet then season with pepper. Stir for a few minutes until the kale is wilted and tender.
- Transfer the sautéed kale to a serving dish then enjoy warm.

Day 11

Breakfast : Sweet Apple Pancake

Lunch : Healthy Shrimps in Sour Sauce

Dinner : Mushroom Refreshing Soup

Sweet Apple Pancake

Serving: 4

Nutrition Facts
Serving Size 4 (103g)
Per Serving
Calories 120
Total Fat 6.9g
Saturated Fat 5.5g
Trans Fat 0g
Cholesterol 41mg
Sodium 33mg
Potassium 115mg
Total Carb 12.9g
Dietary Fiber 4.4g
Sugars 6.9g
Protein 2.9g
Nutrition Facts
Serving Size 4 (103g)
Per Serving
Calories 120

Ingredients:

1-teaspoon coconut oil

1 apple

1 cup grated apple

½ teaspoon cinnamon

1 organic egg

4 tablespoon almond milk

2 tablespoons coconut flour

A pinch nutmeg

Directions:

- Peel the apple and discard the seeds.
- Cut the apple into dices and let it sit.
- Preheat saucepan, pour in coconut oil.
- Once it is hot, stir in diced apple then sauté until wilted. Transfer the apple to a container then set aside.
- Crack an egg over the grated apple.
- Pour almond milk into the bowl and stir until incorporated.
- In another bowl, combine cinnamon, nutmeg, and coconut flour. Mix well.
- Add dry and liquid mixture, stir with a whisker until completely combined.
- Preheat the saucepan again and once it is hot, pour a spoon of the mixture then cook for a few minutes. Make sure that both sides of the pancakes are well cooked.
- Repeat to the remaining mixture then arranges the pancakes on a serving dish.
- Top the pancakes with cooked diced apples then serve immediately.

Healthy Shrimps in Sour Sauce

Serving: 4

Nutrition Facts
Servings: 4
Per Serving
Calories 180
Total Fat 7.5g
Saturated Fat 2.4g
Trans Fat 0g
Cholesterol 210mg
Sodium 274mg
Potassium 325mg
Total Carb 4.9g
Dietary Fiber 1.7g
Sugars 1.2g
Protein 22.7g
Nutrition Facts
Servings: 4
Per Serving
Calories 180

Ingredients:

2 tablespoons coconut oil

1 tablespoon minced garlic

¼ cup chopped onion

1 lb. medium shrimps

2 cups broccoli florets

2 medium carrots

½ cup vegetable broth

½ cup tomato puree

Directions:

- Peel and discard the shrimps' head. Set aside.
- Cut the carrot into stick and place in a bowl. Set aside.
- Preheat a wok over medium heat then pour coconut oil into it.
- Once the oil is hot, stir in chopped onion and sautés until wilted and aromatic.
- Next, add shrimps into the wok and stir until the color of the shrimps are pink.
- Pour vegetable broth into the wok and bring to boil.
- Once it is boiled, stir in broccoli florets and carrots into the wok and bring to a simmer while stirring occasionally.
- The last, stir in tomato puree into the wok and cook until just boiled.
- Transfer the shrimps together with the vegetables to a serving dish then serve warm.

Mushroom Refreshing Soup

Serving: 4

Nutrition Facts
Servings: 4
Per Serving
Calories 66
Total Fat 1.8g
Saturated Fat 0.5g
Trans Fat 0g
Cholesterol 0mg
Sodium 973mg
Potassium 382mg
Total Carb 5.3g
Dietary Fiber 1.4g
Sugars 3g
Protein 6.7g
Nutrition Facts
Servings: 4
Per Serving
Calories 66

Ingredients:

2 cups chopped mushroom

1 cup chopped organic chicken

¼ cup chopped leek

5 cups vegetable broth

¼ teaspoon pepper

¼ teaspoon nutmeg

1 tablespoon chopped onion

Directions:

- Pour vegetable broth in a pot.
- Add chopped onion into the pot then bring to boil.
- Once it is boiled, stir in mushroom and chicken into the pot then season with pepper and nutmeg.
- Stir the soup occasionally and bring to a simmer for about 3 minutes.
- When the vegetables are wilted and cooked, remove from heat then transfer the soup to serving bowl.
- Sprinkle chopped leek over the soup then stirs a little—the heat will make the leek wilted.
- Serve and enjoy hot.

Day 12

Breakfast : Super Banana Porridge

Lunch : Chicken Casserole

Dinner : Mixed Stuffed Eggplant

Super Banana Porridge

Serving: 3

Nutrition Facts
Serving Size 3 (160g)
Per Serving

Calories 256
Total Fat 19.2g
Saturated Fat 17g
Trans Fat 0g
Cholesterol 0mg
Sodium 12mg
Potassium 348mg
Total Carb 23.1g
Dietary Fiber 4.7g
Sugars 14.1g
Protein 2.8g
Nutrition Facts
Serving Size 3 (160g)

Per Serving
Calories 256

Ingredients:

¾ cup mashed banana

1 medium ripe banana

1 cup almond milk

86

1-teaspoon cinnamon

Directions:

- Combine mashed banana and almond milk in a bowl. Stir until mixed and smooth.
- Divide the mashed banana mixture into three serving bowls then dust cinnamon over the banana.
- Peel the ripe banana then cut into slices.
- Sprinkle sliced banana on top as garnish then serve immediately.

Chicken Casserole

Serving: 12

Nutrition Facts
Servings: 12
Per Serving
Calories 181
Total Fat 11.5g
Saturated Fat 7.6g
Trans Fat 0g
Cholesterol 145mg
Sodium 74mg
Potassium 181mg
Total Carb 1.8g
Dietary Fiber 0.7g
Sugars 1g
Protein 17.7g
Nutrition Facts
Servings: 12
Per Serving
Calories 181

Ingredients:

4 cups chopped chicken

2 tablespoons coconut oil

1-cup coconut milk

8 organic eggs

¼ cup coconut flour

1-teaspoon nutmeg

1-teaspoon cinnamon

Directions:

- Place the chopped chicken in a food processor then process until becoming crumbles. Set aside.
- Preheat an oven to 350 F then greases a casserole dish with cooking spray. Set aside.
- Preheat a saucepan over low heat then add coconut oil and coconut flour into the pan. Whisk until mixed.
- Slowly pour coconut milk over the flour then stirs until thickened. Remove from heat.
- Crack the eggs then separate the egg yolks and whites.
- Whisk the egg yolks then pour into the coconut milk mixture then season with nutmeg and cinnamon.
- Add chicken into the mixture and mix well. Set aside.
- In a different bowl, whisk the egg whites until fluffy then stir into the chicken mixture. Stir until combined.
- Pour the batter to the prepared casserole dish then spread evenly.
- Bake for about 20 minutes or until the top of the casserole is lightly brown.
- Once it is done, remove from the oven and serve warm

Mixed Stuffed Eggplant

Serving: 4

Nutrition Facts
Serving Size 4 (194g)
Per Serving
Calories 128
Total Fat 3.1g
Saturated Fat 1.5g
Trans Fat 0g
Cholesterol 44mg
Sodium 41mg
Potassium 423mg
Total Carb 7.7g
Dietary Fiber 4.1g
Sugars 3.8g
Protein 17.9g
Nutrition Facts
Serving Size 4 (194g)
Per Serving
Calories 128

Ingredients:

4 large eggplants

½ lb. cooked chicken

1-teaspoon coconut oil

1 cup diced zucchini

¼ cup chopped onion

½ teaspoon pepper

Celeries, for garnish

Directions:

- Shred the cooked chicken then place in a bowl.
- Preheat a skillet over medium heat then pour coconut oil into it.
- Once it is hot, stir in chopped onion then sautés until wilted and aromatic.
- Add shredded chicken into the skillet then pour coconut milk over the skillet. Stir until the coconut milk is completely absorbed into the chicken.
- Season with pepper then keeps stirring until the chicken is completely seasoned.
- Add diced zucchini into the skillet then mix until just combined. Remove from the heat.
- Preheat an oven to 400 °F then lines a baking sheet with parchment paper. Set aside.
- Horizontally, cut the eggplants into halves then fill each eggplant with cooked chicken.
- Arrange the filled eggplants on the prepared baking sheet then bake for about 15 minutes and once it is done, take them out from the oven.
- Transfer the stuffed tomatoes on a serving dish.
- Serve and enjoy warm.

Day 13

Breakfast : Baked Sweet Potato

Lunch : Gluten Free Blueberry Muffins

Dinner : Eggplant in Flavorful Yellow Sauce

Baked Sweet Potato

Serving: 4

Nutrition Facts
Servings: 2
Per Serving
Calories 44
Total Fat 0g
Saturated Fat 0g
Trans Fat 0g
Cholesterol 0mg
Sodium 26mg
Potassium 5mg
Total Carb 10.7g
Dietary Fiber 2.1g
Sugars 1.9g
Protein 0.8g
Nutrition Facts
Servings: 2
Per Serving
Calories 44

Ingredients:

¾ lb. medium sweet potatoes

1-teaspoon cinnamon

92

Directions:

- Preheat an oven to 400 °F.
- Wash the sweet potatoes then place on a baking sheet.
- Bake the sweet potato for about 50 minutes until it cracks—bigger sweet potatoes will take longer time to cook.
- Once it cracks, take the baked sweet potatoes out from the oven and transfer to a serving dish.
- Sprinkle cinnamon over the sweet potatoes then enjoy warm.

Blueberry Almond Muffins

Serving: 7

Nutrition Facts
Servings: 7
Per Serving
Calories 188
Total Fat 17.2g
Saturated Fat 7.7g
Trans Fat 0g
Cholesterol 23mg
Sodium 11mg
Potassium 58mg
Total Carb 4.6g
Dietary Fiber 2.2g
Sugars 1.7g
Protein 1.2g
Nutrition Facts
Servings 7
Per Serving
Calories 188

Ingredients:

1 cup almond flour

½ cup almond milk

2 tablespoons coconut oil

1 organic egg

4 tablespoons fresh blueberries

Directions:

- Preheat an oven to 350 F and grease 7 muffin cups with cooking spray. Set aside.

- Place the almond milk and coconut oil in a bowl then crack the egg and place in the same bowl. Mix until incorporated.
- Gently pour the liquid mixture into the almond flour then using a rubber spatula stir the mixture until completely combined.
- Stir in fresh blueberries then mix until just combined.
- Divide the mixture into 7 muffin cups then bake for about 25 minutes or until a toothpick inserted comes out clean.
- Once it is done, take the muffins out from the oven and let them cool for a few minutes.
- Serve right away or place in a container with a lid and chill in the refrigerator.
- Enjoy cool if you want to.
- The muffins can be chilled up to 5 days.

Eggplant in Flavorful Yellow Sauce

Serving: 4

Nutrition Facts
Servings: 8
Per Serving

Calories 249
Total Fat 18.4g
Saturated Fat 14.2g
Trans Fat 0g
Cholesterol 45mg
Sodium 191mg
Potassium 217mg
Total Carb 4.8g
Dietary Fiber 1.8g
Sugars 2.7g
Protein 18.6g
Nutrition Facts
Servings: 8

Per Serving
Calories 249

Ingredients:

3 medium eggplants

1 cup chopped kale

1 tablespoon sliced shallot

½ teaspoon curry

½ teaspoon pepper

2 cups coconut milk

1-teaspoon coconut oil

Directions:

- Cut the eggplants into thick slices. You don't need to peel them. Set aside.
- Preheat a wok over medium heat then pour coconut oil into it.
- Once it is hot, stir in sliced shallot then sautés until aromatic.
- Add curry into the wok then toss in eggplants then stir vigorously.
- Pour coconut milk into the wok then sprinkle pepper on top. Bring to boil then cook the eggplants for a few minutes.
- After that, stir in chopped kale into the wok. Stir until the kale is just wilted.
- Transfer to a serving bowl then enjoy hot.

Day 14

Breakfast : Sweet Potato Cup Cakes

Lunch : Single Turkey Patty

Dinner : Soft Green Spinach

Sweet Potato Cupcakes

Serving: 4

Nutrition Facts
Serving Size 4 (85g)
Per Serving
Calories 101
Total Fat 2.2g
Saturated Fat 1.1g
Trans Fat 0g
Cholesterol 41mg
Sodium 32mg
Potassium 191mg
Total Carb 20.1g
Dietary Fiber 3.3g
Sugars 13g
Protein 2.1g
Nutrition Facts
Serving Size 4 (85g)
Per Serving
Calories 101

Ingredients:

¼ cup mashed sweet potato

2 ½ tablespoons grated carrot

2 tablespoons grated coconut

2 tablespoons grated apple

½ teaspoon cinnamon powder

¼ teaspoon nutmeg

1 organic egg

Directions:

- Preheat an oven to 350 °F then greases 4 muffin cups with cooking oil. Set aside.
- Place the mashed sweet potato in a medium bowl then adds grated carrot, grated coconut, and grated apple into it.
- Using your hand, mix those ingredients until well mixed then seasons with cinnamon powder and nutmeg.
- Crack the egg on the mixture and continue mix until completely combined.
- Divide the mixture into 4 prepared cupcake cups and bake for about 30 minutes until the cupcakes are completely done.
- Remove from the oven and take them out from the cupcake cups.
- Serve and enjoy warm.

Single Patty Turkey

Serving: 1

Nutrition Facts
Serving Size 1 (198g)
Per Serving
Calories 282
Total Fat 17.2g
Saturated Fat 6g
Trans Fat 0g
Cholesterol 249mg
Sodium 144mg
Potassium 179mg
Total Carb 3.8g
Dietary Fiber 1.1g
Sugars 1.3g
Protein 27.7g
Nutrition Facts
Serving Size 1 (198g)
Per Serving
Calories 282

Ingredients:

½ cup organic ground turkey

1 organic egg

1 teaspoon minced garlic

½ teaspoon pepper

1 ½ teaspoons almond meal

½ teaspoon coconut oil

Tomato wedges, for garnish

Directions:

- Place ground turkey in a bowl then season with minced garlic and pepper. Stir well.
- Add almond meal into the mixture then using your hand, combine the mixture.
- Next, crack the egg and drop it over the turkey then mix until completely combined.
- After that, shape the mixture into patty form then let it sit in the refrigerator for about 5 minutes.
- Meanwhile, preheat a pan over low heat then pour coconut oil into it.
- Place the patty on the pan then cooks for about 4 minutes then flip it.
- Cook the patty for another 4 minutes until both sides are brown and completely cooked.
- Transfer the cooked patty on a serving dish then garnish with tomato wedges.
- Serve and enjoy warm.

Soft Green Spinach

Serving: 2

Nutrition Facts
Serving Size 4 (96g)
Per Serving
Calories 35
Total Fat 1.2g
Saturated Fat 1g
Trans Fat 0g
Cholesterol 0mg
Sodium 82mg
Potassium 188mg
Total Carb 5.9g
Dietary Fiber 2g
Sugars 3.2g
Protein 1g

Nutrition Facts
Serving Size 4 (96g)
Per Serving
Calories 35

Ingredients:

1 ½ cups sliced spinach

2 teaspoons sliced shallot

¼ teaspoon pepper

1-teaspoon coconut oil

Directions:

- Preheat a skillet then pour coconut oil into it.
- Once it is hot, stir in sliced shallot then sautés until lightly brown.

- Next, add chopped spinach into the skillet then season with pepper. Stir until the spinach is wilted and tender. Do not cook for too long.
- Transfer the cooked spinach to a serving dish then enjoy warm.

Day 15

Breakfast : Spinach Baked Egg

Lunch : Mixed Salads in Halved Avocado

Dinner : Fish Ball Soup

Spinach Baked Egg

Serving: 2

Nutrition Facts
Serving Size 2 (64g)
Per Serving

Calories 72
Total Fat 5g
Saturated Fat 1.9g
Trans Fat 0g
Cholesterol 164mg
Sodium 68mg
Potassium 131mg
Total Carb 1.2g
Dietary Fiber 0.4g
Sugars 0.7g
Protein 5.9g
Nutrition Facts
Serving Size 2 (64g)

Per Serving
Calories 72

Ingredients:

2 organic eggs

½ cup chopped spinach

2 tablespoons diced tomato

¼ teaspoon pepper

¼ teaspoon coconut oil

Directions:

- Preheat an oven to 400 °F then brushes two muffin cups with coconut oil. Set aside.
- Crack the eggs then place in a bowl.
- Season with pepper then add chopped spinach and diced tomatoes. Stir well.
- Pour the egg mix into the prepared muffin cups then bake for 15 minutes.
- Once it is done, remove the baked egg from the oven then let them warm for a few minutes.
- Serve and enjoy warm.

Mixed Salads in Halved Avocado

Serving: 4

Nutrition Facts
Serving Size 4 (139g)
Per Serving
Calories 215
Total Fat 19.7g
Saturated Fat 4.2g
Trans Fat 0g
Cholesterol 0mg
Sodium 49mg
Potassium 572mg
Total Carb 10.9g
Dietary Fiber 7.3g
Sugars 1.8g
Protein 2.2g
Nutrition Facts
Serving Size 4 (139g)
Per Serving
Calories 215

Ingredients:

2 ripe avocados

¼ cup steamed sliced carrots

¼ cup chopped cabbage

¼ cup chopped lettuce

¼ cup tomato wedges

2 tablespoons lemon juice

Directions:

- Cut the avocados into halves then discard the seeds.

- Take the avocado flesh out and let the avocado becoming bowls.
- Cut the avocado flesh into small cubes then place in a bowl together with carrots, cabbage, lettuce, and tomato.
- Drizzle lemon juice over the salads then using two forks, mix them until combined.
- Fill the avocado bowl with the vegetable mixture then arrange on a serving dish.
- Serve and enjoy right away.

Fish Ball Soup

Serving: 4

Nutrition Facts
Serving Size 6 (220g)

Per Serving

Calories 210
Total Fat 10.4g
Saturated Fat 2.7g
Trans Fat 0g
Cholesterol 26mg
Sodium 795mg
Potassium 362mg
Total Carb 15.3g
Dietary Fiber 1.3g
Sugars 0.6g
Protein 14.5g
Nutrition Facts
Serving Size 6 (220g)

Per Serving
Calories 210

Ingredients:

1 lb. fish fillet

1-tablespoon coconut flour

1 organic egg white

2 teaspoons minced garlic

3 cups vegetable broth

½ teaspoon pepper

¼ teaspoon nutmeg

1 tablespoon chopped leek

Directions:

- Place the fish fillet in a food processor together with coconut flour and a teaspoon of minced garlic. Pulse the processor until the fish fillet becoming smooth mixture.
- Transfer the mixture to a bowl then add egg white into it. Using your hand, mix until combined.
- Shape the mixture into small balls form then set aside.
- Pour vegetable broth into a pot then season with nutmeg and pepper. Bring to boil.
- Once it is boiled, add the fish balls into the pot then cook until the balls floating.
- Transfer the cook fish ball together with the gravy to the bowl then sprinkle chopped leek on top.
- Serve and enjoy hot.

Day 16

Breakfast : Soft Coco Banana

Lunch : Stir Fry Kale

Dinner : Sour Chicken Wings Tomato

Soft Coco Banana

Serving: 2

Nutrition Facts
Serving Size 4 (210g)
Per Serving
Calories 448
Total Fat 38.4g
Saturated Fat 27.1g
Trans Fat 0g
Cholesterol 0mg
Sodium 22mg
Potassium 516mg
Total Carb 27g
Dietary Fiber 5.8g
Sugars 13.6g
Protein 6.8g
Nutrition Facts
Serving Size 4 (210g)
Per Serving
Calories 448

Ingredients:

¾ cup mashed banana

½ cup chopped roasted cashew

½ cup almond flour

110

1 medium ripe banana

2 cups coconut milk

1-teaspoon cinnamon

Directions:

- Combine mashed banana, roasted cashew, and almond flour in a bowl. Stir until mixed.
- Divide the mashed banana mixture into three serving bowls then pour coconut milk over the banana.
- Peel the ripe banana then cut into slices.
- Sprinkle sliced banana on top as garnish then serve immediately.

Stir Fry Chinese cabbage

Serving: 2

Nutrition Facts
Servings: 2
Per Serving
Calories 147
Total Fat 14.3g
Saturated Fat 11.9g
Trans Fat 0g
Cholesterol 0mg
Sodium 251mg
Potassium 264mg
Total Carb 3.9g
Dietary Fiber 1.2g
Sugars 1.7g
Protein 2.7g
Nutrition Facts
Servings: 2
Per Serving
Calories 147

Ingredients:

2 tablespoons coconut oil

1 teaspoon minced garlic

¼ cup chopped onion

1 teaspoon red chili flakes

2 cups chopped Chinese cabbage

½ cup vegetable broth

Directions:

- Preheat a skillet over medium heat then pour coconut oil into it.

- Once the oil is hot, stir in chopped onion and sautés until wilted and aromatic.
- Next, add beef red chili flakes into the skillet and stir until wilted.
- Toss in chopped Chinese cabbage into the skillet then mix until the cabbage is completely seasoned.
- Pour vegetable broth into the skillet and bring to boil.
- Cook until the cabbage is cooked enough but still crispy.
- Transfer the cooked cabbage to a serving dish then serve warm.

Sour Chicken Wings Tomato

Serving: 5

Nutrition Facts
Servings: 5
Calories 223
Total Fat 8.7g
Saturated Fat 3.4g
Trans Fat 0g
Cholesterol 81mg
Sodium 101mg
Potassium 575mg
Total Carb 8.2g
Dietary Fiber 1.5g
Sugars 3.6g
Protein 27.7g
Nutrition Facts

Per Serving
Calories 223

Ingredients:

1 lb. chicken wings

2 cloves garlic

3 tablespoons chopped shallot

2 teaspoons coconut oil

½ cup water

1 ½ cup tomato puree

Directions:

- Place garlic, shallot, and red chilies in a food processor then pulse until smooth.

114

- Preheat a wok over medium heat then pour coconut oil into it.
- Once it is hot, stir in the garlic, shallot, and chilies mixture into the wok. Sauté until aromatic.
- Pour water into the wok then add the chicken wings into it.
- Stir occasionally then brings to boil until the water is reduced into half and the chicken wings are completely seasoned.
- Pour tomato puree into the skillet then bring to boil while stirring occasionally.
- When the chicken wings are completely cooked, transfer to a serving dish together with the tomato sauce.
- Serve and enjoy right away.

Day 17

Breakfast : Coconut Tomato Pancake

Lunch : Raw Salmon Fritter

Dinner : Simple Broccoli Brownie

Coconut Tomato Pancake

Serving: 4

Nutrition Facts

Serving Size 4 (136g)

Per Serving

Calories 124
Total Fat 8.6g
Saturated Fat 7g
Trans Fat 0g
Cholesterol 41mg
Sodium 44mg
Potassium 263mg
Total Carb 9.4g
Dietary Fiber 4.1g
Sugars 3.5g
Protein 3.6g
Nutrition Facts

Serving Size 4 (136g)

Per Serving
Calories 124

Ingredients:

1-teaspoon coconut oil

½ cup diced tomato

½ cup tomato puree

¼ cup coconut flakes

1 organic egg

4 tablespoons coconut milk

2 tablespoons coconut flour

Directions:

- Preheat a saucepan then pour coconut oil into it.
- Once it is hot, stir in diced tomato then sauté until wilted.
- Add tomato puree into the saucepan then stir until completely cooked. Transfer the tomato to a container then set aside.
- Place coconut flakes in a bowl then crack an egg and place in the same bowl.
- Pour coconut milk into the bowl and stir until incorporated.
- Stir in coconut flour then using a whisker stir the mixture until completely combined.
- Preheat the saucepan again and once it is hot, pour a spoon of the mixture then cook for a few minutes. Make sure that both sides of the pancakes are well cooked.
- Repeat to the remaining mixture then arranges the pancakes on a serving dish.
- Top the pancakes with tomato sauce then serve immediately.

Raw Salmon Fritter

Serving: 4

Nutrition Facts
Serving Size 4 (214g)
Per Serving
Calories 255
Total Fat 13g
Saturated Fat 3.9g
Trans Fat 0g
Cholesterol 214mg
Sodium 128mg
Potassium 518mg
Total Carb 5.9g
Dietary Fiber 2.8g
Sugars 1g
Protein 28.8g
Nutrition Facts
Serving Size 4 (214g)
Per Serving
Calories 255

Ingredients:

1 lb. salmon fillet

4 organic eggs

2 tablespoons chopped leek

1 tablespoon minced garlic

1 ½ teaspoon pepper

2 tablespoons coconut flour

½ teaspoon coconut oil

Directions:

- Place salmon in a food processor then process until smooth.
- Transfer the salmon to a bowl then seasons with minced garlic and pepper. Stir well.
- Add coconut flour and chopped leek into the mixture then using your hand, combine the mixture.
- Next, crack the egg and drop it over the salmon mixture then mix until completely combined.
- After that, shape the mixture into medium patty form then let it sit in the refrigerator for about 5 minutes.
- Meanwhile, preheat a pan over low heat then pour coconut oil into it.
- Place the salmon fritters on the pan then cooks for about 4 minutes then flip it.
- Cook for another 4 minutes until both sides are brown and completely cooked.
- Transfer the cooked salmon fritter on a serving dish.
- Serve and enjoy immediately.

Simple Broccoli Brownie

Serving: 4

Nutrition Facts
Serving Size 4 (96g)
Per Serving
Calories 35
Total Fat 1.2g
Saturated Fat 1g
Trans Fat 0g
Cholesterol 0mg
Sodium 82mg
Potassium 188mg
Total Carb 5.9g
Dietary Fiber 2g
Sugars 3.2g
Protein 1g
Nutrition Facts
Serving Size 4 (96g)
Per Serving
Calories 35

Ingredients:

3 cups broccoli florets

¼ cup minced garlic

¼ teaspoon pepper

1-teaspoon coconut oil

Directions:

- Preheat a skillet then pour coconut oil into it.
- Once it is hot, stir in minced garlic then sautés until wilted and aromatic.

- Next, add broccoli florets into the skillet then season with pepper. Keep stirring until the broccoli is wilted and tender.
- Let the broccoli stay on the heat while stirring them occasionally until the broccoli is brown.
- Transfer the cooked broccoli to a serving dish then enjoy warm.

Day 18

Breakfast : Tasty Scrambled Eggs with Zucchini

Lunch : Red Green Salads

Dinner : Beef Crystal Soup

Tasty Scrambled Eggs with Zucchini

Serving: 1

Nutrition Facts
Servings: 1

Per Serving

Calories 179
Total Fat 11.4g
Saturated Fat 4.8g
Trans Fat 0g
Cholesterol 327mg
Sodium 143mg
Potassium 645mg
Total Carb 7.9g
Dietary Fiber 2.4g
Sugars 4.1g
Protein 13.6g
Nutrition Facts

Per Serving
Calories 179

Ingredients:

½ teaspoon coconut oil

1 medium zucchini

2 organic eggs

½ teaspoon black pepper

Directions:

- Cut the zucchini into halves then discard the seeds.
- After that, cut the zucchini into small cubes then set aside.
- Crack the organic eggs then place on a bowl.
- Season with pepper then stir well.
- Preheat a saucepan over medium heat then pour coconut oil into it.
- Add chopped bell pepper into the saucepan then stir until wilted.
- Pour the beaten egg into the saucepan then quickly scramble the egg.
- After that, add zucchini cubes into the saucepan then stir until just combined.
- Transfer the scrambled egg to a serving dish then enjoy warm

Red Green Salads

Serving: 4

Nutrition Facts
Servings: 4
Per Serving
Calories 150
Total Fat 10.3g
Saturated Fat 2.2g
Trans Fat 0g
Cholesterol 0mg
Sodium 23mg
Potassium 549mg
Total Carb 15.1g
Dietary Fiber 4.9g
Sugars 7.8g
Protein 2.6g
Nutrition Facts
Servings: 4
Per Serving
Calories 150

Ingredients:

1 ripe avocado

3 cups watermelon cubes

2 cups chopped parsley

2 tablespoons lemon juice

¼ teaspoon black pepper

Directions:

- Peel the avocado then discard the seed. Cut the avocado into cubes then place in a salad bowl.

- Add chopped parsley and watermelon cubes into the bowl then drizzle lemon juice over the salad.
- Sprinkle black pepper on top then using two forks mixes all of the ingredients until well combined.
- Chill in the refrigerator for at least an hour then enjoy whenever you want.

Beef Crystal Soup

Serving: 4

Nutrition Facts
Servings: 4
Per Serving
Calories 148
Total Fat 4.5g
Saturated Fat 1.5g
Trans Fat 0g
Cholesterol 38mg
Sodium 1003mg
Potassium 586mg
Total Carb 5.9g
Dietary Fiber 1.2g
Sugars 3.2g
Protein 19.5g
Nutrition Facts
Servings: 4
Per Serving
Calories 148

Ingredients:

2 cups chopped grass-fed beef

1 cup chopped carrots

¼ cup chopped leek

5 cups vegetable broth

¼ teaspoon pepper

¼ teaspoon nutmeg

1 tablespoon chopped onion

½ cup chopped tomato

Directions:

- Pour vegetable broth in a pot.
- Add chopped onion into the pot then bring to boil.
- Once it is boiled, stir in beef into the pot then season with pepper and nutmeg.
- Cover the pot with its lid then reduce the heat. Cook for about 20 minutes until the beef is tender.
- Add chopped carrots into the pot then cook again for about 3 minutes.
- When the carrots are wilted and cooked, toss in chopped tomatoes then bring to a simmer for about a minute.
- Remove the soup from heat then transfer to serving bowl.
- Sprinkle chopped leek over the soup then stirs a little—the heat will make the leek wilted.
- Serve and enjoy hot.

Day 19

Breakfast : Warm Green Smoothie

Lunch : Coconut Cinnamon Muffins

Dinner : Roasted Chicken Wings Black Pepper

Warm Green Smoothie

Serving: 4

Nutrition Facts
Servings: 2
Per Serving
Calories 132
Total Fat 0.5g
Saturated Fat 0.1g
Trans Fat 0g
Cholesterol 0mg
Sodium 33mg
Potassium 758mg
Total Carb 32.7g
Dietary Fiber 4.1g
Sugars 21.8g
Protein 2.4g
Nutrition Facts
Servings: 2
Per Serving
Calories 132

Ingredients:

1 fresh green apple

1 medium cucumber

1 tablespoon lemon juice

128

1-teaspoon ginger

1 cup chopped kale

1-cup fresh coconut water

Directions:

- Cut the apple and discard the seeds then place in a blender.
- Cut the cucumber into four pieces then add them to the blender
- Add chopped kale into the blender then splash lemon juice over the vegetables and stir ginger in.
- Pulse the blender on high for about 20 seconds until smooth.
- Divide the smoothie into two glasses then serve immediately.

Coconut Cinnamon Muffins

Serving: 7

Nutrition Facts
Servings: 4

Calories 177
Total Fat 17.2g
Saturated Fat 14.5g
Trans Fat 0g
Cholesterol 41mg
Sodium 28mg
Potassium 114mg
Total Carb 5g
Dietary Fiber 2.7g
Sugars 1.7g
Protein 2.8g
Nutrition Facts

Per Serving
Calories 177

Ingredients:

1-cup coconut flour

½ cup coconut milk

2 tablespoons coconut oil

1 organic egg

4 tablespoons coconut flakes

1-teaspoon cinnamon

Directions:

- Preheat an oven to 350 F and grease 7 muffin cups with cooking spray. Set aside.

- Place the coconut milk and coconut oil in a bowl then crack the egg and place in the same bowl. Mix until incorporated.
- Gently pour the liquid mixture into the almond flour then using a rubber spatula stir the mixture until completely combined.
- Stir in fresh blueberries then mix until just combined.
- Divide the mixture into 7 muffin cups then bake for about 25 minutes or until a toothpick inserted comes out clean.
- Once it is done, take the muffins out from the oven and let them cool for a few minutes.
- Serve right away or place in a container with a lid and chill in the refrigerator.
- Enjoy cool if you want to.
- The muffins can be chilled up to 5 days.

Roasted Chicken Wings Black Pepper

Serving: 4

Nutrition Facts
Servings: 4
Per Serving

Calories 229
Total Fat 9.7g
Saturated Fat 3.3g
Trans Fat 0g
Cholesterol 101mg
Sodium 101mg
Potassium 295mg
Total Carb 0.9g
Dietary Fiber 0.3g
Sugars 0g
Protein 33g
Nutrition Facts
Servings: 4
Per Serving
Calories 229

Ingredients:

1 lb. organic chicken wings

1-teaspoon coconut oil

¼ teaspoon cumin

¼ teaspoon oregano

1 teaspoon minced garlic

½ teaspoon chili powder

1-teaspoon black pepper

Directions:

- Combine cumin with oregano, chili pepper, and minced garlic in a bowl.
- Pour coconut oil into the spices then mix until becoming wet mixture.
- Rub the chicken wings with the spice mixture then let it sit for about 10 minutes.
- Wrap the seasoned chicken wings with aluminum foil then place in a baking sheet.
- Preheat an oven to 300 °F and once it is ready, place the baking sheet with wrapped chicken wings in the oven. Bake for about 40 minutes.
- When the process is done, remove the chicken wings from the oven and carefully unwrap the chicken wings.
- Place the baked chicken wings on a serving dish then sprinkle black pepper on top.
- Serve and enjoy warm.

Day 20

Breakfast : Spinach and Broccoli Omelet

Lunch : Simple Steamed Carrots

Dinner : Hot Beef Balls

Spinach and Broccoli Omelet

Serving: 4

Nutrition Facts
Serving Size 1 (131g)
Per Serving

Calories 177
Total Fat 13.4g
Saturated Fat 6.7g
Trans Fat 0g
Cholesterol 327mg
Sodium 138mg
Potassium 243mg
Total Carb 3.2g
Dietary Fiber 1.1g
Sugars 1.4g
Protein 12g
Nutrition Facts
Serving Size 1 (131g)
Per Serving
Calories 177

Ingredients:

2 organic eggs

1-teaspoon coconut oil

1-tablespoon cup chopped onion

¼ cup chopped spinach

¼ cup chopped broccoli

¼ teaspoon pepper

Directions:

- Crack the eggs then place into a bowl.
- Season with pepper then whisk until incorporated.
- Add chopped spinach and broccoli into the bowl then mix well.
- Next, preheat a saucepan over medium heat then pour coconut oil into it.
- Once it is hot, stir in chopped onion and sautés until wilted.
- Pour the egg mixture over the saucepan then cook until sets.
- Once it is cooked, transfer the omelet to a serving platter then enjoy!

Simple Steamed Carrots

Serving: 4

Nutrition Facts
Serving Size 4 (136g)
Per Serving

Calories 54
Total Fat 0.1g
Saturated Fat 0.1g
Trans Fat 0g
Cholesterol 0mg
Sodium 91mg
Potassium 419mg
Total Carb 12.5g
Dietary Fiber 3.2g
Sugars 6.2g
Protein 1.1g
Nutrition Facts
Serving Size 4 (136g)

Per Serving
Calories 54

Ingredients:

8 medium red carrots

¼ cup chopped celery

2 tablespoons lemon juice

½ teaspoon pepper

Directions:

- Peel the carrots then shred until becoming long noodle.
- Place the shredded carrots in a steamer then steam for a few minutes until tender.

- Transfer the steamed carrots to a salad bowl then add chopped celery into the bowl.
- Drizzle lemon juice and sprinkle pepper over the carrots.
- Using two forks mix the steamed carrots with other ingredients until combined.
- Chill in the refrigerator for at least an hour.
- Enjoy anytime you want.

Hot Beef Balls

Serving: 4

Nutrition Facts
Serving Size 6 (232g)
Per Serving

Calories 200
Total Fat 12.5g
Saturated Fat 5.3g
Trans Fat 0g
Cholesterol 47mg
Sodium 439mg
Potassium 120mg
Total Carb 2.9g
Dietary Fiber 1.3g
Sugars 0.6g
Protein 17.9g
Nutrition Facts
Serving Size 6 (232g)
Per Serving
Calories 200

Ingredients:

1 lb. grass-fed ground beef

1-tablespoon coconut flour

1 organic egg white

2 teaspoons minced garlic

3 cups beef broth

½ teaspoon pepper

¼ teaspoon nutmeg

1 tablespoon chopped leek

½ cup chopped vegetable mustard

Directions:

- Place the ground beef in a food processor together with coconut flour and a teaspoon of minced garlic. Pulse the processor until smooth.
- Transfer the mixture to a bowl then add egg white into it. Using your hand, mix until combined.
- Shape the mixture into medium balls form then set aside.
- Pour vegetable broth into a pot then season with nutmeg and pepper. Bring to boil.
- Once it is boiled, add the meatballs into the pot then cook until the balls floating.
- Add chopped vegetable mustard into the pot then stirs until just wilted.
- Transfer the cook meatballs together with the gravy to the bowl then sprinkle chopped leek on top.
- Serve and enjoy hot.

Day 21

Breakfast : Pumpkin Creamy Puree

Lunch : Cabbage Salads with Tomato

Dinner : Spicy Chicken Curry

Pumpkin Creamy Puree

Serving: 4

Nutrition Facts
Serving Size 4 (177g)
Per Serving

Calories 297
Total Fat 28.8g
Saturated Fat 25.5g
Trans Fat 0g
Cholesterol 0mg
Sodium 21mg
Potassium 435mg
Total Carb 11.7g
Dietary Fiber 4.6g
Sugars 5.9g
Protein 3.4g
Nutrition Facts
Serving Size 4 (177g)

Per Serving
Calories 297

Ingredients:

2 cups coconut milk

1-teaspoon cinnamon

½ lb. pumpkin

140

Directions:

- Peel and cut the pumpkin then place in a steamer.
- Steam the pumpkin for a few minutes until the pumpkin is soft.
- Place the pumpkin in a food processor then add coconut milk and cinnamon into it.
- Pulse the food processor and process the food until smooth and creamy.
- Transfer the smooth mixture into four serving bowls then serve immediately.

Cabbage Salads with Tomato

Serving: 4

Nutrition Facts
Serving Size 4 (96g)
Per Serving

Calories 35
Total Fat 1.2g
Saturated Fat 1g
Trans Fat 0g
Cholesterol 0mg
Sodium 82mg
Potassium 188mg
Total Carb 5.9g
Dietary Fiber 2g
Sugars 3.2g
Protein 1g
Nutrition Facts
Serving Size 4 (96g)
Per Serving
Calories 35

Ingredients:

3 cups chopped cabbage

½ cup red tomato wedges

¼ cup chopped onion

1 tablespoon chopped celery

¼ teaspoon pepper

1-teaspoon coconut oil

Directions:

- Preheat a skillet then pour coconut oil into it.

- Once it is hot, stir in chopped onion then sautés until wilted and aromatic.
- Next, add chopped cabbage into the skillet then season with pepper. Keep stirring until the cabbage is wilted and tender.
- After that, add tomato wedges and celeries into the skillet then using a wooden spatula, mix all of them until combined and wilted.
- Transfer the cabbage salads to a serving dish then enjoy warm.

Spicy Chicken Curry

Serving: 4

Nutrition Facts
Serving Size 3 (220g)
Per Serving
Calories 347
Total Fat 23.8g
Saturated Fat 9.4g
Trans Fat 0g
Cholesterol 235mg
Sodium 140mg
Potassium 268mg
Total Carb 5.5g
Dietary Fiber 1.2g
Sugars 2.7g
Protein 27.9g
Nutrition Facts
Serving Size 3 (220g)
Per Serving
Calories 347

Ingredients:

¾ lb. organic chicken breast

3 organic eggs

¼ teaspoon nutmeg

¼ teaspoon ginger

1 ½ teaspoons almond meal

½ teaspoon coconut oil

½ teaspoon vegetable oil

1 teaspoon minced garlic

2 teaspoons sliced shallot

1-teaspoon curry powder

144

1 tablespoon red chili flakes

¼ teaspoon pepper

1 ½ cups coconut milk

Directions:

- Cut the chicken breast into cubes then place in a food processor together with nutmeg, ginger, and almond meal.
- Transfer the chicken mixture to a bowl then add eggs over the mixture then stir until completely combined.
- After that, shape the mixture into small balls form then let them sit in the refrigerator for about 5 minutes.
- Meanwhile, preheat a pan over low heat then pour coconut oil into it.
- Place the chicken balls on the pan then cooks for about 4 minutes then flip it.
- Cook the chicken balls for another 4 minutes until both sides are brown and completely cooked. Set aside.
- Next, preheat a skillet over medium heat then pour vegetable oil into it.
- Stir in minced garlic, sliced shallot, and red chili flakes then sautés until translucent and aromatic.
- Pour water into the skillet then add curry powder into it.
- After that, add the chicken balls into the skillet and stir until the chicken balls are completely seasoned.

- Pour the coconut milk over the chicken balls; stir for a few minutes then brings to a simmer.
- Transfer the chicken balls along with the gravy to a serving dish.
- Serve and enjoy warm.

Day 22

Breakfast : Special Spinach Frittata

Lunch : Beef Tomato Burritos

Dinner : Mixed Veggie in Red

Special Spinach Frittata

Serving: 4

Nutrition Facts
Serving Size 4 (136g)
Per Serving
Calories 229
Total Fat 19.3g
Saturated Fat 12g
Trans Fat 0g
Cholesterol 327mg
Sodium 134mg
Potassium 251mg
Total Carb 3.4g
Dietary Fiber 1g
Sugars 2g
Protein 12.1g
Nutrition Facts
Serving Size 4 (136g)
Per Serving
Calories 229

Ingredients:

1-tablespoon coconut oil

1 cup chopped spinach

¼ cup chopped onion

8 organic eggs

½ cup coconut milk

¼ teaspoon pepper

Directions:

- Preheat an oven to 350 °F.
- Crack the organic eggs then place in a bowl.
- Add pepper and coconut milk into the eggs then using a whisker whisk the eggs until completely beaten. Set aside.
- Preheat a non-stick skillet over medium heat then pour coconut oil into it.
- Once it is hot, stir in chopped onion then sautés until lightly brown and aromatic.
- Next, add chopped spinach into the skillet then stir until wilted.
- Pour the egg mixture into the skillet then place the skillet in the oven.
- Bake for about 15 minutes until the egg is completely cooked.
- Remove the frittata from the oven then transfer to a serving platter.
- Serve and enjoy immediately.

Beef Tomato Burritos

Serving: 2

Nutrition Facts
Serving Size 2 (154g)
Per Serving
Calories 175
Total Fat 9.5g
Saturated Fat 3.6g
Trans Fat 0g
Cholesterol 201mg
Sodium 102mg
Potassium 142mg
Total Carb 3.2g
Dietary Fiber 0.7g
Sugars 1.6g
Protein 17.5g
Nutrition Facts
Serving Size 2 (154g)
Per Serving
Calories 175

Ingredients:

2 organic eggs

2 tablespoons water

¼ teaspoon pepper

½ teaspoon coconut oil

FILLING:

½ cup grass-fed ground beef

¼ cup chopped onion

1 teaspoon minced garlic

¼ cup halved cherry tomatoes

149

Directions:

- Crack the organic eggs then place in a bowl.
- Using a whisker, whisk the eggs until beaten.
- Preheat a skillet over medium heat then brushes with coconut oil.
- Once it is hot, pour half of the beaten eggs then swirl until it spreads evenly.
- Cook until set then flip it.
- Once both sides of the egg are completely cooked, remove it from the pan.
- Repeat with the remaining egg mixture then set aside.
- Preheat a saucepan then stir in chopped onion and minced garlic into the pan. Sautés until wilted and aromatic.
- Add ground beef and cherry tomatoes into the pan then mix until combined and the beef is completely cooked.
- Place the eggs on a flat surface then drop about two scoops of filling on top.
- Roll them tightly and place on a serving platter.
- Serve and enjoy warm.

Mixed Veggie in Red

Serving: 10

Nutrition Facts
Serving Size 10 (198g)
Per Serving

Calories 215
Total Fat 12.6g
Saturated Fat 7.1g
Trans Fat 0g
Cholesterol 22mg
Sodium 48mg
Potassium 553mg
Total Carb 5.6g
Dietary Fiber 1.9g
Sugars 3.4g
Protein 20.5g
Nutrition Facts
Serving Size 10 (198g)
Per Serving
Calories 215

Ingredients:

5 large red tomatoes

4 cups cooked tuna

2 teaspoons coconut oil

1 cup coconut milk

¼ cup chopped onion

½ teaspoon pepper

1 ½ cup chopped spinach

½ cup chopped cabbage

Directions:

- Preheat a skillet over medium heat then pour coconut oil into it.
- Once it is hot, stir in chopped onion then sautés until wilted and aromatic.
- Add tuna into the skillet then pour coconut milk over the skillet. Stir until the coconut milk is completely absorbed into the tuna.
- Season with pepper then keeps stirring until the tuna is completely seasoned.
- Stir in chopped spinach and cabbage then mix until just combined. Remove the filling from the heat.
- Preheat an oven to 400 °F then lines a baking sheet with parchment paper. Set aside.
- Horizontally, cut the top of the tomatoes into halves then discard the pulp until the tomatoes becoming small bowls.
- Fill each tomato with cooked tuna then arranges on the prepared baking sheet.
- Bake the filled tomatoes for about 15 minutes and once it is done, take them out from the oven.
- Transfer the stuffed tomatoes on a serving then serve and enjoy warm.

Day 23

Breakfast : Savory Green Pancake

Lunch : Cauliflower Chicken Muffin

Dinner : Asian Egg Sambal

Savory Green Pancake

Serving: 4

Nutrition Facts
Serving Size 4 (107g)
Per Serving

Calories 126
Total Fat 9.6g
Saturated Fat 7.3g
Trans Fat 0g
Cholesterol 82mg
Sodium 50mg
Potassium 124mg
Total Carb 6.2g
Dietary Fiber 3.4g
Sugars 1.7g
Protein 4.5g
Nutrition Facts
Serving Size 4 (107g)
Per Serving
Calories 126

Ingredients:

1-teaspoon coconut oil

½ cup chopped zucchini

¼ cup coconut flakes

153

2 organic eggs

¼ cup coconut milk

2 tablespoons coconut flour

Directions:

- Preheat a saucepan then pour coconut oil into it.
- Place coconut flakes in a bowl then crack the eggs and place in the same bowl.
- Pour coconut milk into the bowl and stir until incorporated.
- Stir in coconut flour then using a whisker stir the mixture until completely combined.
- Preheat the saucepan again and once it is hot, pour a spoon of the mixture then sprinkle chopped zucchini on it.
- Cook for a few minutes. Make sure that both sides of the pancakes are well cooked.
- Repeat to the remaining mixture then arranges the pancakes on a serving dish.
- Top the pancakes with tomato sauce then serve immediately.

Cauliflower Chicken Muffins

Serving: 6

Nutrition Facts
Serving Size 6 (151g)
Per Serving

Calories 114
Total Fat 4.6g
Saturated Fat 2.8g
Trans Fat 0g
Cholesterol 91mg
Sodium 73mg
Potassium 103mg
Total Carb 9.1g
Dietary Fiber 5.4g
Sugars 1.6g
Protein 8.5g
Nutrition Facts
Serving Size 6 (151g)
Per Serving
Calories 114

Ingredients:

6 tablespoons coconut flour

1 cup chopped cauliflower

½ cup cooked chicken

3 organic eggs

½ teaspoon nutmeg powder

¼ teaspoon pepper

½ teaspoon lemon juice

Directions:

- Preheat an oven to 350 °F then greases 6 muffin cups. Set aside.
- Cut the cooked chicken into small dices then set aside.
- Place all ingredients in a bowl then using a whisker, combine until incorporated.
- Divide the mixture into 6 prepared muffin cups then bake for about 25 minutes until the muffins are set and completely cooked.
- Once it is done, remove from the oven then let them cool.
- Serve and enjoy.

Asian Eggs Sambal

Serving: 5

Nutrition Facts
Servings: 5
Per Serving
Calories 98
Total Fat 6.3g
Saturated Fat 3g
Trans Fat 0g
Cholesterol 164mg
Sodium 65mg
Potassium 150mg
Total Carb 5.3g
Dietary Fiber 0.8g
Sugars 1g
Protein 6.1g
Nutrition Facts
Servings: 5
Per Serving
Calories 98

Ingredients:

5 organic eggs

2 cloves garlic

5 cloves shallot

10 red chilies

½ teaspoon turmeric

2 teaspoons lemon grass

2 teaspoons crumbled bay leaves

2 teaspoons coconut oil

¼ cup water

Directions:

- Pour water into a pot then place organic eggs into it.
- Bring to boil and once it is boiled, let the eggs stay until completely boiled.
- Remove the pot from heat then discard the water.
- Pour cold water into the pot and let the eggs sit for about 10 minutes. The boiled eggs will be easier to be peeled off.
- Meanwhile, place garlic, shallot, and red chilies in a food processor then pulse until smooth.
- Preheat a wok over medium heat then pour coconut oil into it.
- Once it is hot, stir in the garlic, shallot, and chilies mixture into the wok together with turmeric, lemon grass, and bay leaves. Sauté until aromatic.
- Pour water into the wok then add boiled eggs into it.
- Stir occasionally then brings to a simmer until the water is completely absorbed into the eggs.
- When it is done, transfer to a serving dish then enjoys.

Day 24

Breakfast : Avocado Creamy Smoothie

Lunch : Egg Spinach Salads

Dinner : Baked Salmon Original

Avocado Creamy Smoothie

Serving: 4

Nutrition Facts
Servings: 4
Per Serving
Calories 266
Total Fat 24.2g
Saturated Fat 14.8g
Trans Fat 0g
Cholesterol 0mg
Sodium 15mg
Potassium 503mg
Total Carb 13.8g
Dietary Fiber 5.5g
Sugars 5.5g
Protein 2.7g
Nutrition Facts
Servings: 4
Per Serving
Calories 266

Ingredients:

1 cup almond milk

¾ cup ice cubes

1 ripe avocado

1 small banana

2 tablespoons lemon juice

½ teaspoon cinnamon

Directions:

- Cut the avocado into halves then discards the seed.
- Scoop out the avocado flesh then place in a blender.
- Peel the banana then add into the blender.
- Splash lemon juice then sprinkles cinnamon over the ingredients.
- Blend all of the ingredients on high for about 20 minutes until smooth.
- Transfer the smoothie to a serving dish then enjoy right away.

Egg Spinach Salads

Serving: 2

Nutrition Facts
Servings: 2
Per Serving
Calories 164
Total Fat 7.2g
Saturated Fat 1.8g
Trans Fat 0g
Cholesterol 164mg
Sodium 91mg
Potassium 398mg
Total Carb 19.9g
Dietary Fiber 3.6g
Sugars 12.5g
Protein 7.4g
Nutrition Facts
Servings: 2
Per Serving
Calories 164

Ingredients:

2 organic eggs

1 fresh green apple

2 cups chopped spinach

2 tablespoons minced garlic

1-teaspoon olive oil

2 tablespoons lemon juice

Directions:

- Preheat a saucepan then pour olive oil into it.

- Once it is hot, stir in minced garlic then sautés until lightly brown. Set aside.
- Pour water in a pot then put the eggs into it. Bring to boil then cook the eggs until completely boiled.
- Transfer the eggs to a bowl with cold water and let them cool.
- Cut the fresh apple into wedges and discard the seeds.
- Place the apple wedges and spinach in a salad dish then drizzles lemon juice on top.
- Peel the eggs and cut into wedges. Add the egg wedges over the spinach and apples then sprinkle sautéed garlic on top.
- Serve and enjoy right away.

Baked Salmon Original

Serving: 3

Nutrition Facts
Servings: 3
Per Serving
Calories 166
Total Fat 8.6g
Saturated Fat 2.3g
Trans Fat 0g
Cholesterol 50mg
Sodium 51mg
Potassium 449mg
Total Carb 0.7g
Dietary Fiber 0.2g
Sugars 0g
Protein 22.1g
Nutrition Facts
Servings: 3
Per Serving
Calories 166

Ingredients:

¾ lb. salmon fillet

1-teaspoon coconut oil

¼ teaspoon cumin

¼ teaspoon oregano

½ teaspoon pepper

1 teaspoon minced garlic

Directions:

- Place cumin, oregano, pepper, and minced garlic in a bowl.

- Pour olive oil into the spices then mix until becoming wet mixture.
- Rub the salmon with the spice mixture then let it sit for about 8 minutes.
- Wrap the salmon with aluminum foil then place in a baking sheet.
- Preheat an oven to 250 °F and once it is ready, place the baking sheet with wrapped chicken wings in the oven. Bake for about 40 minutes.
- After 40 minutes, remove the baked salmon from the oven and carefully unwrap it.
- Transfer the baked salmon on a serving dish then enjoys warm.

Day 25

Breakfast : Baked Broccoli Creamy

Lunch : Avocado Shrimp Salads

Dinner : Spinach Coconut Soup

Baked Broccoli Creamy

Serving: 12

Nutrition Facts
Servings: 12

Per Serving

Calories 122

Total Fat 9.8g

Saturated Fat 6.4g

Trans Fat 0g

Cholesterol 136mg

Sodium 63mg

Potassium 191mg

Total Carb 4.2g

Dietary Fiber 1.4g

Sugars 1.8g

Protein 5.9g

Nutrition Facts

Servings: 12

Per Serving

Calories 122

Ingredients:

3 cups broccoli florets

3 teaspoons coconut oil

1-cup coconut milk

10 organic eggs

¼ cup coconut flour

1-teaspoon nutmeg

1-teaspoon pepper

1 cup chopped onion

Directions:

- Preheat an oven to 350 F then greases a casserole dish with cooking spray. Set aside.
- Preheat a saucepan over low heat then add coconut oil and coconut flour into the pan. Whisk until mixed.
- Slowly pour coconut milk over the flour then stirs until thickened. Remove from heat.
- Crack the eggs then separate the egg yolks and whites.
- Whisk the egg yolks then pour into the coconut milk mixture then season with nutmeg and pepper.
- Add broccoli and chopped onion into the mixture and mix well. Set aside.
- In a different bowl, whisk the egg whites until fluffy then stir into the broccoli mixture. Stir until combined.
- Pour the batter to the prepared casserole dish then spread evenly.
- Bake for about 20 minutes or until the top of the casserole is lightly brown.

- Once it is done, remove from the oven and serve warm or cold.
- You can make it the night before and keep in the refrigerator.

Avocado Shrimp Salads

Serving: 2

Nutrition Facts
Serving Size 2 (115g)
Per Serving
Calories 216
Total Fat 19.7g
Saturated Fat 4.1g
Trans Fat 0g
Cholesterol 36mg
Sodium 106mg
Potassium 487mg
Total Carb 8.9g
Dietary Fiber 6.7g
Sugars 0.8g
Protein 4.4g
Nutrition Facts
Serving Size 2 (115g)
Per Serving
Calories 216

Ingredients:

1 ripe avocado

½ cup small shrimps

Directions:

- Remove the shrimps' heads and peel the skin then wash and rinse them.
- Place the shrimps in a steamer then steam them for two minutes only—don't over steam them.
- Take the shrimps out from the steamer then set aside.

- Cut the ripe avocado into halves and discard the seed.
- Scoop out the avocado flesh then using a spoon mash the avocado until smooth.
- Cut half of the shrimps into pieces then add them into the mashed avocado. Mix well.
- Divide the mashed avocado into two then garnishes with the remaining shrimps.
- Serve and enjoy immediately.

Spinach Coconut Soup

Serving: 4

Nutrition Facts
Servings: 4
Per Serving
Calories 184
Total Fat 15g
Saturated Fat 12.8g
Trans Fat 0g
Cholesterol 0mg
Sodium 146mg
Potassium 1137mg
Total Carb 11.2g
Dietary Fiber 5.2g
Sugars 2.7g
Protein 6.5g
Nutrition Facts
Servings: 4
Per Serving
Calories 184

Ingredients:

2 bunches fresh spinach

1 teaspoon sliced garlic

3 tablespoons sliced shallot

½ teaspoon coriander

2 teaspoons crumbled bay leaves

1-½ cups water

1-cup coconut milk

Directions:

- Chop the spinach then washes them. Set aside.
- Place sliced garlic, shallot, coriander, and bay leaves in a pot.
- Pour water into the pot then bring boil.
- Once it is boiled, add chopped spinach into the pot.
- Add coconut milk into the pot then bring to a simmer for about 2 minutes while stirring occasionally.
- Transfer the spinach coconut soup to a serving bowl then enjoy hot.

Day 26

Breakfast	:	Sweet Potato Soufflé
Lunch	:	Zucchini Green Fritter
Dinner	:	Appetizing Beef Stew

Sweet Potato Soufflé

Serving: 6

Nutrition Facts
Servings: 6

Per Serving

Calories 161
Total Fat 10.1g
Saturated Fat 7.6g
Trans Fat 0g
Cholesterol 82mg
Sodium 76mg
Potassium 173mg
Total Carb 14.1g
Dietary Fiber 3g
Sugars 3.5g
Protein 4.8g
Nutrition Facts

Servings: 6

Per Serving
Calories 211

Ingredients:

1 cup mashed sweet potato

1-tablespoon coconut oil

½ cup coconut milk

3 organic eggs

2 tablespoons coconut flour

½ teaspoon nutmeg

½ teaspoon cinnamon

Directions:

- Preheat an oven to 350 F then greases a small soufflé dish with cooking spray. Set aside.
- Preheat a saucepan over low heat then add coconut oil and coconut flour into the pan. Whisk until mixed.
- Slowly pour coconut milk over the flour then stirs until thickened. Remove from heat.
- Crack the eggs then separate the egg yolks and whites.
- Whisk the egg yolks then pour into the coconut milk mixture then season with nutmeg and cinnamon.
- Add mashed sweet potato into the mixture and mix well. Set aside.
- In a different bowl, whisk the egg whites until fluffy then stir into the sweet potato mixture. Stir until combined.
- Pour the batter to the prepared soufflé dish then spread evenly.
- Bake for about 30 minutes or until the top of the soufflé is lightly brown, serve warm,

Zucchini Green Fritter

Serving: 3

Nutrition Facts
Serving Size 3 (344g)
Per Serving
Calories 211
Total Fat 13.6g
Saturated Fat 2.8g
Trans Fat 0g
Cholesterol 164mg
Sodium 92mg
Potassium 800mg
Total Carb 13g
Dietary Fiber 5.1g
Sugars 5.1g
Protein 12.3g
Nutrition Facts
Serving Size 3 (344g)
Per Serving
Calories 211

Ingredients:

3 medium zucchini

3 organic eggs

2 tablespoons chopped leek

1-cup broccoli florets

1 tablespoon minced garlic

2 tablespoons almond flour

½ teaspoon coconut oil

Directions:

- Peel the zucchini then cut into cubes.

174

- Place cubed zucchini and broccoli florets in a food processor then process until smooth.
- Transfer the zucchini and broccoli mixture to a bowl then seasons with minced garlic. Stir well.
- Add almond flour flour and chopped leek into the mixture then using your hand, combine the mixture.
- Next, crack the egg and drop it over the zucchini and broccoli mixture then mix until completely combined.
- After that, shape the mixture into medium patty form then let it sit in the refrigerator for about 5 minutes.
- Meanwhile, preheat a pan over low heat then pour coconut oil into it.
- Place the zucchini fritters on the pan then cooks for about 4 minutes then flip it.
- Cook for another 4 minutes until both sides are brown and completely cooked.
- Transfer the cooked zucchini fritter on a serving dish.
- Serve and enjoy immediately.

Appetizing Beef Stew

Serving: 8

Nutrition Facts
Servings: 8
Per Serving
Calories 249
Total Fat 18.4g
Saturated Fat 14.2g
Trans Fat 0g
Cholesterol 45mg
Sodium 191mg
Potassium 217mg
Total Carb 4.8g
Dietary Fiber 1.8g
Sugars 2.7g
Protein 18.6g
Nutrition Facts
Serving: 8
Per Serving
Calories 249

Ingredients:

1 lb. grass-fed beef chunks

1 cup chopped cabbage

1 medium red tomato

1 tablespoon sliced shallot

½ teaspoon curry

½ teaspoon pepper

2 cups coconut milk

1-teaspoon coconut oil

Directions:

- Preheat a wok over medium heat then pour coconut oil into it.
- Once it is hot, stir in sliced shallot then sautés until aromatic.
- Add curry into the wok then toss in beef chunks then stir vigorously.
- Once the beef is seasoned, add chopped cabbage into the wok and mix well.
- Pour coconut milk into the wok then sprinkle pepper on top. Bring to boil then reduce the heat and cook the beef until tender.
- Cut the tomato into wedges then add into the wok. Stir until the tomato wedges just wilted.
- Transfer to a serving bowl then enjoy hot.

Day 27

Breakfast : Scrambled Egg in Tomato Pool

Lunch : Energizing Baked Pineapple

Dinner : Pork Chops with Cinnamon

Scrambled Egg in Tomato Pool

Serving: 1

Nutrition Facts
Servings: 1
Per Serving
Calories 196
Total Fat 11.6g
Saturated Fat 4.8g
Trans Fat 0g
Cholesterol 327mg
Sodium 137mg
Potassium 724mg
Total Carb 11.7g
Dietary Fiber 3.3g
Sugars 7.4g
Protein 13.4g
Nutrition Facts
Servings
Per Serving
Calories 196

Ingredients:

½ teaspoon coconut oil

2 organic eggs

½ teaspoon black pepper

2 medium red tomatoes

1 tablespoon chopped leek

Directions:

- Crack the organic eggs then place on a bowl.
- Season with pepper then stir well.
- Preheat a saucepan over medium heat then pour coconut oil into it.
- Add chopped bell pepper into the saucepan then stir until wilted.
- Pour the beaten egg into the saucepan then quickly scramble the egg.
- Remove the scrambled egg from the heat then set aside.
- Place the red tomatoes in a steamer then steam until soft.
- Cut the steamed tomatoes into wedges then place them in a saucepan.
- Preheat the saucepan over low heat while stirring occasionally until the tomatoes are wilted and watery.
- Stir in scrambled eggs then mix until just combined.
- Transfer the scrambled egg to a serving dish together with the tomato gravy then sprinkle chopped leek on top.
- Serve and enjoy warm

Energizing Baked Pineapple

Serving: 2

Nutrition Facts
Servings: 2

Calories 193
Total Fat 2.7g
Saturated Fat 0.4g
Trans Fat 0g
Cholesterol 0mg
Sodium 189mg
Potassium 423mg
Total Carb 36.9g
Dietary Fiber 7g
Sugars 25.3g
Protein 5.2g
Nutrition Facts

Per Serving
Calories 193

Ingredients:

1 ripe pineapple

2 ripe oranges

1 cup chopped spinach or any greens, as you desired

1-teaspoon olive oil

Directions:

- Preheat an oven to 350 °F then lines a baking sheet with aluminum foil.
- Peel then cut the pineapple into slices.

- Brush each slice of the pineapple with olive oil then place on the lined baking sheet.
- Bake the pineapples for about 10 minutes then carefully flip them.
- Brush the other side of the pineapple with olive oil then bakes again for about 10 minutes or until both sides of the pineapple are brown.
- Place chopped spinach and orange on the serving dish
- Add baked pineapple on the top then serve and enjoy.

Pork Chops with Cinnamon

Serving: 1

Nutrition Facts
Servings: 4
Per Serving
Calories 171
Total Fat 4.5g
Saturated Fat 1.5g
Trans Fat 0g
Cholesterol 83mg
Sodium 65mg
Potassium 500mg
Total Carb 1.1g
Dietary Fiber 0.5g
Sugars 0g
Protein 29.8g
Nutrition Facts
Servings: 4
Per Serving
Calories 171

Ingredients:

1 lb. chopped pork

½ teaspoon cumin

1-½ teaspoons minced garlic

¼ teaspoon pepper

1-teaspoon cinnamon

1 tablespoon avocado oil

Directions:

- Place cumin, minced garlic, pepper, and cinnamon in a bowl. Mix well.
- Rub the chopped pork with the spice mixture then chill in the refrigerator for about an hour.
- After an hour, take the seasoned pork out from the refrigerator and let it sit in the room temperature for about 15 minutes.
- Meanwhile, preheat a cast iron skillet over medium heat.
- Once it is hot, brush the skillet with avocado oil then place the seasoned pork on the skillet.
- Cook the chopped pork for about 4-8 minutes or until it is brown and ready to flip.
- Flip the pork and cook again for another 5 minutes or until both sides of the pork are brown and completely cooked.
- Transfer the cooked pork to a serving dish then enjoy warm.

Day 28

Breakfast : Onion Thick Pancake

Lunch : Refreshing Tropical Salads

Dinner : Grilled Fish with Tropical Sauce

Onion Thick Pancake

Serving: 4

Nutrition Facts

Serving Size 4 (136g)

Per Serving

Calories 124
Total Fat 8.6g
Saturated Fat 7g
Trans Fat 0g
Cholesterol 41mg
Sodium 44mg
Potassium 263mg
Total Carb 9.4g
Dietary Fiber 4.1g
Sugars 3.5g
Protein 3.6g
Nutrition Facts

Serving Size 4 (136g)

Per Serving
Calories 124

Ingredients:

1-teaspoon coconut oil

184

1 cup chopped green onion

½ cup chopped cabbage

1 tablespoon chopped parsley

¼ cup coconut flakes

2 organic eggs

¼ cup coconut milk

2 tablespoons coconut flour

Directions:

- Preheat a saucepan then pour coconut oil into it.
- Place coconut flakes in a bowl then crack the eggs and place in the same bowl.
- Pour coconut milk into the bowl and stir until incorporated.
- Stir in coconut flour then using a whisker stir the mixture until completely combined.
- Add chopped onion, chopped cabbage, and chopped parsley into the mixture then mix well.
- Preheat the saucepan again and once it is hot, pour a spoon of the mixture cooks for a few minutes. Make sure that both sides of the pancakes are well cooked.
- Repeat to the remaining mixture then arranges the pancakes on a serving dish.
- Top pancakes with tomato sauce and serve.

Refreshing Tropical Salads

Serving: 4

Nutrition Facts

Servings: 2

Per Serving
Calories 154
Total Fat 0.6g
Saturated Fat 0.2g
Trans Fat 0g
Cholesterol 0mg
Sodium 5mg
Potassium 542mg
Total Carb 39g
Dietary Fiber 5.4g
Sugars 26.2g
Protein 2.2g

Nutrition Facts
Servings: 2
Per Serving

Ingredients:

- 1 cup green apple cubes
- 1 cup chopped orange
- 1 cup sliced banana
- 1 cup chopped pineapple
- 2 tablespoon lemon juice

Directions:

- Place apple, orange, banana, and pineapple in container with a lid.
- Drizzle lemon juice over the fruits then using two forks mix until well combined.
- Cover the container with the lid and chill in the refrigerator for at least 2 hours.

186

- Once you want to consume, remove from the refrigerator and enjoy immediately.

Grilled Fish with Tropical Sauce

Serving: 2

Nutrition Facts
Servings: 6
Per Serving
Calories 169
Total Fat 8g
Saturated Fat 2.6g
Trans Fat 0g
Cholesterol 48mg
Sodium 81mg
Potassium 286mg
Total Carb 8.4g
Dietary Fiber 1.6g
Sugars 4.6g
Protein 15.7g
Nutrition Facts
Servings: 6
Per Serving
Calories 169

Ingredients:

1 lb. fresh fish

1 tablespoon minced garlic

2 tablespoons lemon juice

SAUCE:

1-cup tomato puree

½ cup chopped tomato

½ cup chopped carrot

½ cup chopped pineapple

¼ cup chopped leek

2 tablespoons chopped onion

1-teaspoon coconut oil

½ cup water

Directions:

- Rub the fish with minced garlic then drizzles lemon juice over the fish. Set aside.
- Preheat a grill over medium heat then place the fish on it. Grill until the fish is completely cooked.
- Meanwhile, cook the sauce.
- Preheat a saucepan over medium heat then pour coconut oil into it.
- Once it is hot, stir in chopped onion then sautés until aromatic and lightly golden brown.
- Next, add carrot and leek into the pan and stir until wilted.
- Pour tomato puree together with water then brings to boil.
- Once it is boiled, stir in chopped tomatoes and pineapples then bring to a simmer for about 3 minutes.
- When the fish is well cooked, place it on a serving dish then drizzles the sauce over the fish.
- Serve and enjoy warm.

Day 29

Breakfast : Pure Pumpkin Smoothie

Lunch : Mixed Fruit Salad in Asian Sauce

Dinner : Cauliflower Rice

Pure Pumpkin Smoothie

Serving: 4

Nutrition Facts
Servings: 2
Per Serving
Calories 255
Total Fat 24.7g
Saturated Fat 19.3g
Trans Fat 0g
Cholesterol 0mg
Sodium 10mg
Potassium 461mg
Total Carb 10.3g
Dietary Fiber 4.3g
Sugars 5.1g
Protein 2.5g
Nutrition Facts
Servings: 2
Per Serving
Calories 255

Ingredients:

½ cup coconut milk

¾ cup mashed pumpkin

1-teaspoon cinnamon

3 teaspoons coconut oil

¼ cup cubed avocado

Directions:

- Place mashed pumpkin and avocado in a blender.
- Pour coconut milk and coconut oil into the blender then blend until smooth.
- Once it is done, transfer the pumpkin smoothie to a serving glass.
- Serve and enjoy right away or chill in the refrigerator if you want to consume it later.

Mixed Fruit Salads in Asian Sauce

Serving: 4

Nutrition Facts
Servings: 4
Per Serving
Calories 190
Total Fat 8.5g
Saturated Fat 1.7g
Trans Fat 0g
Cholesterol 0mg
Sodium 7mg
Potassium 413mg
Total Carb 28.8g
Dietary Fiber 3.6g
Sugars 19.6g
Protein 4g
Nutrition Facts
Servings: 4
Per Serving
Calories 190

Ingredients:

1 red apple

1 mango

1 medium cucumber

SAUCE:

½ cup chopped cashew

½ teaspoon minced garlic

¼ teaspoon tamarind

1 teaspoon red chili flakes

¾ cup water

Directions:

- Make the sauce first.
- Place all of the sauce ingredients in a blender then blend until incorporated. Set aside.
- Chop the apple, mango, and cucumber into thin slices then place in salad bowl.
- Pour the sauce over the fruits then mix well.
- Refrigerate for about an hour then serve cold.

Cauliflower Rice

Serving: 4

Nutrition Facts
Servings: 4
Per Serving
Calories 75
Total Fat 4.4g
Saturated Fat 3.7g
Trans Fat 0g
Cholesterol 0mg
Sodium 22mg
Potassium 258mg
Total Carb 8.8g
Dietary Fiber 2.8g
Sugars 3.6g
Protein 1.9g
Nutrition Facts
Servings: 4
Per Serving
Calories 75

Ingredients:

2 cups cauliflower florets

1 cup chopped cabbage

½ cup chopped leek

3 teaspoons coconut oil

2 teaspoons minced garlic

2 tablespoons coconut flakes

1 cup chopped onion

Directions:

- Place the cauliflower florets in a food processor then pulse until the cauliflower florets becoming crumbled.
- Preheat coconut oil in a large frying pan over medium heat.
- Once the oil is hot, stir in minced garlic and onion then sauté until aromatic and lightly brown.
- Next, add chopped cabbage and leek into the pan then sauté until wilted.
- After that, stir in cauliflower and coconut flakes then stir until combined and completely cooked.
- Transfer the cooked cauliflower rice to a serving dish.
- Serve and enjoy right away.

Day 30

Breakfast : Mushroom Frittata Veggie

Lunch   : Chicken Greenie Salads

Dinner   : Stir Fry Beef with Broccoli

Mushroom Frittata Veggie

Serving: 4

Nutrition Facts
Serving Size 4 (109g)
Per Serving

Calories 142
Total Fat 9.9g
Saturated Fat 3.7g
Trans Fat 0g
Cholesterol 327mg
Sodium 127mg
Potassium 179mg
Total Carb 1.9g
Dietary Fiber 0.4g
Sugars 1.2g
Protein 11.5g
Nutrition Facts
Serving Size 4 (109g)
Per Serving
Calories 142

Ingredients:

1-teaspoon coconut oil

½ cup chopped mushroom

½ cup chopped spinach

196

¼ cup chopped onion

8 organic eggs

¼ teaspoon pepper

Directions:

- Preheat an oven to 350 °F.
- Crack the organic eggs then place in a bowl.
- Add pepper into the eggs then using a whisker whisk the eggs until completely beaten. Set aside.
- Preheat a non-stick skillet over medium heat then pour coconut oil into it.
- Once it is hot, stir in chopped onion then sautés until lightly brown and aromatic.
- Next, add chopped mushroom and spinach into the skillet then stir until wilted.
- Pour the egg mixture into the skillet then place the skillet in the oven.
- Bake for about 15 minutes until the egg is completely cooked.
- Remove the frittata from the oven then transfer to a serving platter.
- Serve and enjoy immediately.

Chicken Greenie Salads

Serving: 4

Nutrition Facts
Servings: 2
Per Serving
Calories 90
Total Fat 3.7g
Saturated Fat 0.8g
Trans Fat 0g
Cholesterol 27mg
Sodium 34mg
Potassium 151mg
Total Carb 3.3g
Dietary Fiber 1.5g
Sugars 1.4g
Protein 11g
Nutrition Facts
Servings: 2
Per Serving
Calories 90

Ingredients:

½ cup chopped organic chicken

½ cup chopped collard green

1 cup chopped cabbage

1-teaspoon olive oil

½ teaspoon pepper

2 tablespoons lemon juice

Directions:

- Preheat a saucepan over medium heat then pour olive oil into it.
- Once it is hot, stir in chicken into the saucepan and sautés until wilted and no longer oink.
- Season with pepper then cook for a few minutes. Remove from heat then set aside.
- Place the collard green and cabbage in a steamer then steam until wilted. Make sure not to cook it for too long.
- Place the steamed vegetables and cooked chicken in a salad bowl then drizzle lemon juice on top.
- Using two forks mix the salads until combined then serve immediately.

Stir Fry Beef with Broccoli

Serving: 4

Nutrition Facts
Servings: 4
Per Serving
Calories 180
Total Fat 7.5g
Saturated Fat 2.4g
Trans Fat 0g
Cholesterol 210mg
Sodium 274mg
Potassium 325mg
Total Carb 4.9g
Dietary Fiber 1.7g
Sugars 1.2g
Protein 22.7g
Nutrition Facts
Servings: 4
Per Serving
Calories 180

Ingredients:

2 tablespoons avocado oil

1 tablespoon minced garlic

¼ cup chopped onion

1.5 lbs. grass-fed beef chunks

2 cups broccoli florets

½ cup beef broth

Directions:

- Rub the beef chunks with minced garlic and let them sit in the refrigerator for about 30 minutes.

- After 30 minutes, take the beef out from the refrigerator.
- Preheat a wok over medium heat then pour avocado oil into it.
- Once the oil is hot, stir in chopped onion and sautés until wilted and aromatic.
- Next, add beef chunks into the wok and stir until the beef is no longer pink.
- Pour beef broth into the wok and bring to boil.
- Once it is boiled, stir in broccoli florets into the wok and bring to a simmer while stirring occasionally.
- Transfer the beef and broccoli to a serving dish then serve warm.

Made in the USA
Middletown, DE
21 November 2017